Exploring Florida's Gulf Coast Beaches

Help Us Keep This Guide Up to Date

Every effort has been made by the authors and editors to make this guide as accurate and useful as possible. However, many things can change after a guide is published— trails are rerouted, regulations change, techniques evolve, facilities come under new management, etc.

We would love to hear from you concerning your experiences with this guide and how you feel it could be improved and kept up to date. While we may not be able to respond to all comments and suggestions, we'll take them to heart and we'll also make certain to share them with the author. Please send your comments and suggestions to the following address:

The Globe Pequot Press
Reader Response/Editorial Department
P.O. Box 480
Guilford, CT 06437

Or you may e-mail us at:
editorial@globe-pequot.com

Thanks for your input, and happy travels!

A FALCON GUIDE®

Exploring Florida's Gulf Coast Beaches

George Hurchalla

FALCON®

GUILFORD, CONNECTICUT
HELENA, MONTANA

AN IMPRINT OF THE GLOBE PEQUOT PRESS

Text design: Nancy Freeborn
Photo credits: All photos are by the author unless otherwise noted.
Maps by Stefanie Ward © The Globe Pequot Press.

Library of Congress Cataloging-in-Publication Data.

Hurchalla, George.
    Exploring Florida's Gulf Coast Beaches / George Hurchalla.—1st ed.
        p. cm.
    Includes index.
    ISBN 0-7627-1094-2
        1. Gulf Coast (Fla.)—Guidebooks. 2. Beaches—Florida—Gulf Coast—Guidebooks. I. Title. II. Series.

    F317.G8 H87 2002
    917.59'940464—dc21

                                2002032519

Manufactured in the United States of America
First Edition/First Printing

The prices and rates listed in this guidebook were confirmed at press time. We recommend, however, that you call establishments to obtain current information before traveling.

Acknowledgments

My mother and father—for all their love and support
Deirdre and Jonathan Bean—for their hospitality and Gulf help
Clyde Butcher—for a vision that captures the majesty of wild Florida
Florida state parks—for doing such a fine job of preserving old Florida
All the citizens of Florida who fought to preserve and expand public beach access

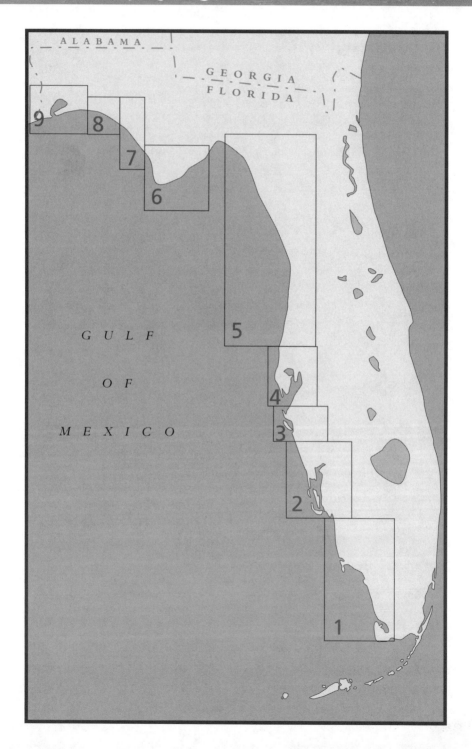

Contents

The Sunshine State xi
How to Use This Book xiii

Region 1 1
    Cape Sable 7
    Ten Thousand Islands 8
    Tigertail Beach County Park 9
    Naples Pier 11
    Lowdermilk Beach 12
    Clam Pass County Park 13
    Delnor-Wiggins Pass State Park 14
    Barefoot Beach Preserve 15
    Lovers Key State Park 17
    Lynn Hall Park aka Pelican Pier 18
    Bowditch Point Regional Park 19
    The Sippi 20

Region 2 21
    Bowman's Beach 26
    Captiva Beach 27
    Cayo Costa State Park 28
    Gasparilla Island State Park 29
    Don Pedro Island State Park 30
    Stump Pass Beach State Park 31
    Englewood Beach 32
    Blind Pass Beach 33
    Manasota Beach 35
    Shelling 36

Region 3 37
    Caspersen Beach 41
    Venice Pier/Brohard Park 42
    North Jetty Beach 43
    Turtle Beach/Palmer Point Beach 44
    Siesta Key Beach Park 46
    Lido Beach/North Lido Beach 48

Coquina Beach/Cortez Beach 49
Manatee Beach 50
Egmont Key State Park 51
Shark's Teeth 53

Region 4 55
Fort De Soto County Park 60
Pass-a-Grille Beach 61
Treasure Island Beach 62
John's Pass Beach/Madeira Beach 62
Tiki Gardens–Indian Shores Access 64
Sand Key County Park 66
Caladesi Island State Park 67
Honeymoon Island State Park 68
Sand Fleas 70

Region 5 71
Howard Park 76
Anclote Keys Preserve State Park 77
Fort Island Beach 79
Cedar Keys National Wildlife Refuge 80
Keaton Beach aka Hodges Park 82
Homosassa or Chassahowitzka? 83

Region 6 . . . .
Dog Island 89
St. George Island State Park 90
Cape St. George State Reserve aka Little St. George 91
St. Vincent National Wildlife Refuge 92
Salinas Park 94
Cape Palms Park 95
St. Joseph Peninsula State Park 97
Never Cry Wolf (Except Here) 99

Region 7 101
Mexico Beach 105
Crooked Island East—Tyndall Air Force Base 106
Crooked Island West—Tyndall Air Force Base 108
St. Andrews State Park and Shell Island 109
Bay County Pier 111
City Pier—Panama City Beach 112

Camp Helen State Park 114
Dolphins 115

Region 8 117
Inlet Beach 121
Deer Lake State Park 121
Grayton Beach State Park 122
Blue Mountain Beach 124
Ed Walline Park 125
Fort Panic Park 126
Topsail Hill State Preserve 127
James Lee County Park 128
Henderson Beach State Park 129
When Is Too Little Too Much? 131

Region 9 133
Eglin Air Force Base 138
Beasley/Brackin Wayside Parks—Okaloosa Island Pier 139
Navarre Beach 141
Opal Beach—Gulf Islands National Seashore 142
Casino Beach 144
Fort Pickens Gate and East Park 144
Langdon Beach/Fort Pickens—Gulf Islands National Seashore 145
Johnson Beach—Gulf Islands National Seashore 147
Perdido Key State Park 148
Ghost Crabs 151

Index 153
About the Author 160

The Sunshine State

At one time or another throughout history, all of Florida has been a beach. During cyclical melting of the polar ice caps, the entire state was underwater up to the beginnings of the Appalachians. Sometimes the narrow central ridge, the only "high" land of the state, was lapped by waves. At other times the state expanded to twice its width, far out into the shallow Gulf of Mexico. Much of the Panhandle was flooded by northern runoff, resulting in today's vast network of rivers and the ever-shifting sands of the gorgeous barrier islands of that region.

Florida's beaches are an ever-changing landscape.

Even more than the east coast, the sands of Florida's Gulf Coast are constantly in flux. Entire coastal towns in the Big Bend have washed away, and passes through the barrier islands of the Gulf have been opened or closed with impunity by storms. The seashells for which the beaches of the southern Gulf are famous are constantly replenished by the vast movements of sand.

The attraction of Florida is that it can be so many things to so many people. It is a constantly evolving landscape, 367 miles wide from Jacksonville to the Alabama border and 426 miles long to the tip of the Florida Keys, encompassing about 770 miles of beaches. In Florida it is never possible to be more than 75 miles from a beach, and 90 percent of the population lives within 10 miles of the ocean!

The Gulf Coast is a much different atmosphere than the Atlantic, with generally placid, shallow waters. Because of the gentle coastal slope, waters fluctuate in temperature much more widely in the Gulf, from bathwater in summer to the Polar Bear Club in winter. Culturally there is greater variance, too, because the Panhandle shares more in common with the American South than the rest of Florida does. From opera in Naples to spring break reveling in Panama City Beach to sea kayaking the miles of "the Saints" wilderness islands, there's something for everyone in the Gulf.

Sea kayaking is a popular way to see the coast.

Exploring Florida's Gulf Coast Beaches is a comprehensive guide to the best beaches of the west coast of Florida, including the Panhandle. Separated into nine regions, beginning at Ten Thousand Islands in the south and ending at Pensacola, the regions can be identified on the overview map of the state (see page vi). Within each region, maps point out the location of each of the area beaches.

An introduction to the region begins each section, giving an overview of the area and differentiating the types of beaches. Local history and other highlights are mentioned. Directions for access from major highways are given. The beaches of the region are listed in south-to-north or east-to-west order, followed by a list of area campsites. The "Other Points of Interest" section details historic sites, museums, zoos, and places of natural wonder close to the beach.

At the end of each section, there are informative essays on a variety of subjects, ranging from local characters to history to creatures of the beach and marine environment.

Beach Safety and Etiquette

Don't kick sand in people's faces! Okay, that's a little too obvious. While beach experiences are generally safe, there are a variety of dangers that you can easily avoid.

First, there's harmful critters: Sea lice are tiny stinging particles, broken jellyfish tentacles or larval jellyfish, that can make some people erupt in painful rashes. See what lifeguard-posted beach condition signs say about whether they're around. Sharks are not a concern along most of the Gulf Coast, but summer months see the bull sharks in migration and it's wise to stay out of the water when any are sighted. "Red tide" is a phenomenon that develops from a bloom of protozoans in especially warm summer waters, resulting in a fish-killing toxin that spreads in waves throughout the Gulf. While generally just a smelly nuisance, it can cause chest problems in more sensitive people.

The Gulf can occasionally kick up dangerous surf during hurricanes and other storms, though most beaches are so shallow near shore that it's hard to get in trouble unless you go swimming out amid the breakers. The greatest dangers are strong tidal currents near inlets and passes, which can sweep a swimmer away easily.

Most Gulf Coast beaches are shallow near shore.

As far as interacting with other humans, it's mostly a case of live-and-let-live. At some wilderness beaches, just be aware that when humans are more than a mile away from other humans they have a propensity to shed their clothes. If this has been a subject of controversy or arrests at any given beach, I mention it. Beyond the building of sand castles, try to leave the beach as you found it, without any litter left behind. Seemingly innocuous things like the plastic holders on six-packs of beverages can tangle in turtles' flippers and kill them.

Beach Ecology

Where natural sand dunes have been left intact (which is most of the Florida coast outside of major urban areas) a protected plant called the sea oat is one of the most important parts of a stable beach. These long stalks wave gently in the breeze, and their roots provide the only resistance beaches have to erosion. In many places the casuarina, or Australian pine, is a common sight along the coast, and over time people have mistakenly associated it as part of old Florida. It is not a native plant, and efforts are being made at most state parks to steadily eradicate it, replacing it with sea grapes and other native species. Hurricane Andrew did this in one fell swoop at Cape Florida, knocking over the park's entire population of Australian pines.

Coquina rock comes and goes in beautiful formations between Jupiter and St. Augustine, an ancient type of rock that was used by the Spanish to construct the oldest fort in Florida, Castillo de San Marcos. In the Florida Keys, beaches are rare because almost all the land is lime rock. On the Gulf beaches, rock is noticeably absent except in human-made structures, which is why the sands shift so dramatically.

Sea turtles make their nests on all Florida beaches in summer months, and after enduring years of decline their numbers are steadily coming back. Raccoons, possums, and bobcats forage along the beach at night, and egrets, blue herons, sandpipers, and ibis hunt for morsels—like sand fleas and ghost crabs—at the water's edge during the day. In parts of the Panhandle, endangered beach mice scurry about the dunes. While at first glance the beach is no more than an expanse of sand, in fact it supports a fascinating and complex ecosystem.

Green sea turtles nest on Florida beaches during the summer months.
PHOTO: NELIA M. COYLE

T he massive Everglades National Park occupies the entire southwestern corner of the state. Much of the Everglades is an inhospitable environment best viewed from the periphery, but if you can deal with the mosquitoes, there are some remote, boat-only beaches fringing the national park that will make you believe you've stepped back a century in time. The beaches of Cape Sable, along with Pavilion Key and other keys of the Ten Thousand Islands, are favorite destinations of adventurous kayakers.

The first sign of civilization coming up out of the Everglades onto the Gulf Coast is Marco Island. Driving State Road 951 to the island feels like traveling to the Florida Keys, the same quiet road through miles of mangrove wilderness. Along the way is the Briggs Nature Center, which is a good place to stop if you want to do some kayaking through the wilds of Rookery Bay or simply some bird-watching from the boardwalk. Marco has undergone a dramatic transformation in the past forty years, from empty wilderness island to a densely developed vacation area, though Tigertail Beach still holds echoes of the former.

Farther north in Naples, the mainland beaches come back for the first time. The town used to be identified only with inland swamps, through the annual swamp buggy races and the multitude of glorious wilderness areas like Corkscrew Swamp Sanctuary, the Fakahatchee, and Big Cypress. Now it has come into its own as a beach resort area, with an upscale downtown and plenty of public access, including the beautiful Clam Pass County Park. Naples even has a philharmonic hall, so along with Fort Myers it is diminishing Sarasota's claim as the only cultural center of southwestern Florida.

The coast between Naples and Fort Myers Beach is still relatively undeveloped; a series of wilderness beaches seem to go on forever. The seclusion and prettiness of these state parks and preserves make them a mecca for folks looking for some solitude. Fort Myers Beach brings civilization back with a bang, being one of the major outlets for the inland population. While some may consider the sprawl of shops a bit on the tacky side, it's definitely the

Clam Pass County Park.

most popular area with younger people because it offers a real social beach scene. From mid-December through Easter, a 25-cent trolley runs from Bowditch Point in Fort Myers Beach down through Lovers Key and all the way to Bonita Beach; hours are 6:30 A.M.–8:00 P.M.

Access

From the east/south—Take I–75 from Fort Lauderdale and get off at exit 15 to Naples/Marco Island, or take the Tamiami Trail (US 41) from Miami to Naples. For the Ten Thousand Islands, take the Everglades City road from the Tamiami Trail.

From the north—Take exit 21 off I–75 west to Fort Myers Beach.

Beaches

Cape Sable
Ten Thousand Islands
Tigertail Beach County Park
Naples Pier
Lowdermilk Beach
Clam Pass County Park
Delnor-Wiggins Pass State Park
Barefoot Beach Preserve
Lovers Key State Park
Lynn Hall Park aka Pelican Pier
Bowditch Point Regional Park

Camping

Everglades National Park/Flamingo Campground—Reservations (800) 365–CAMP, information (305) 242–7700. Located at the end of the main park road in Flamingo, it has 234 drive-in sites, including 55 with a view of the water, 4 group sites, and 64 walk-up sites (20 on the water's edge). Rates are $14 per night. Cold-water showers, two dump stations, picnic tables, grills, an amphitheater for winter programs, and a public telephone. Limited groceries and camping supplies are available at the Flamingo Marina store.

Everglades National Park/Cape Sable and Ten Thousand Islands—Gulf Coast Visitor Center, Everglades City, (941) 695–3311; Flamingo Visitor Center, including all Florida Bay sites, (941) 695–2945. Wilderness camping.

Insect conditions are so severe during summer months that wilderness use is minimal and permit writing desks may not be staffed. Self-registration permits are still required. Winter wilderness users originating from the Florida Keys will be able to obtain permits by phone by calling (941) 695–2945, no more than twenty-four hours prior to the start of their trip, for the following locations only: North Nest Key, Little Rabbit Key, Carl Ross Key, and the Cape Sable Beaches. Fees are $10 for one to six people, $20 for seven to twelve people, $30 for thirteen or more people. Visitor centers are open 7:30 A.M.–5:00 P.M.

Collier-Seminole State Park—(941) 394–3397, Naples. A nice state park along the Tamiami Trail southeast of Naples. A good inland base for visiting Marco Island and Naples beaches, as well as the Fakahatchee and Big Cypress. Rates are $8.00 May through November, $13.00 December through April.

Naples/Marco Island KOA—Reservations (800) 562–7734, information (941) 774–5455. Located in the city of Naples. Just minutes to the beaches of Marco Island and Everglades National Park. Elevated Kamping Kabins, tropical pool, hot tub, canoe rentals, and access to the Gulf of Mexico. Rates are $31–38 for two-person tent sites.

Red Coconut RV Court on the Beach—(941) 463–7200, Fort Myers Beach. The only RV resort in southwestern Florida located right on the beach.

San Carlos RV Park & Islands—(941) 466–3133, in Fort Myers Beach. Swimming pool and heated spa, waterfront picnic area, rec hall, horseshoes, shuffleboard, laundry and showers, public phone, marina/boat ramp, kayak rentals. Pets are permitted with restrictions. For tents or RVs, rates are $25.00–26.00 May through November, $32.50 December through April.

Other Points of Interest

Clyde Butcher Gallery—(941) 695–2428 or (888) 999–9113. Located on the Tamiami Trail near the Fakahatchee State Preserve. An absolute must-stop when crossing the Tamiami Trail. Displays the work of Florida's greatest landscape photographer, whose stunning images of the Everglades, Cayo Costa, and the Loxahatchee River are shot in 8-by-10-inch negative format and blown up to huge prints with incredible detail. Open Wednesday through Saturday 10:00 A.M.–5:00 P.M.

Big Cypress National Preserve—(941) 263–3532, US 41 in Ochopee, about 20 miles south of Naples. Catch a glimpse of herons, bald eagles, deer, and the endangered Florida panther among scenic marshlands.

The Collier County Historical Museum—(941) 774–8476, 3301 Tamiami Trail East, Naples. Highlighting the people, places, and events from the past that helped shape the present in Collier County.

Collier-Seminole State Park—(941) 394–3397, 20200 East Tamiami Trail. Located about 17 miles south of Naples, this park features 6,400 acres of vegetation and wildlife typical of the Everglades. Boat tours, canoe rentals, hiking trail, and a visitor center.

The Conservancy of Southwest Florida's Briggs Nature Center—(941) 775–8569, 401 Shell Island Road. Located off SR 951 in the Rookery Bay National Estuarine Research Reserve and featuring an interpretive center, butterfly garden, boardwalk, and seasonal guided boat tours. Canoe and kayak rentals.

Everglades National Park—(800) 445–7724. The entrance is 25 miles southeast of Naples. The largest protected wilderness east of the Rocky Mountains. A haven for birders, kayakers, nature photographers, and saltwater sportfishermen.

Fakahatchee Strand State Preserve—(941) 695–4593, 7 miles west of SR 29 in Collier County. This 20-mile-long area—part of the Big Cypress Swamp—

is sometimes known as the "orchid capital of the United States" with all forty-four native species of orchids.

Corkscrew Swamp Sanctuary—(941) 657–3771, off Immokalee Road, 20 miles north of Naples and 14 miles west of Immokalee. An 11,000-acre Audubon Society wilderness sanctuary of bald cypress trees hundreds of years old. This spot is home to an array of birds, alligators, bobcats, and otters.

Koreshan State Historic Site—(941) 992–0311, South US 41 at Corkscrew Road near Fort Myers. A nationally recognized historical site, the Koreshan park was a utopian community, settled in the late 1800s. Park rangers offer guided walks and campfire programs according to seasonal demand. The fee is $3.25 per vehicle.

Palm Cottage—(941) 261–8164, 137 12th Avenue South, located by the Naples Pier. Built in 1895, this cottage is the headquarters of the Collier County Historical Society.

The Philharmonic Center for the Arts—(941) 597–1900, 5833 Pelican Bay Boulevard, Naples. A multimillion-dollar headquarters for the performing and fine arts. Includes a gallery and museum shop.

The Teddy Bear Museum of Naples—(941) 598–2711, 2511 Pine Ridge Road, Naples. Home to more than 3,000 teddy bears, from small to giant, plain to fancy, and stuffed to antique.

Matanzas Pass Wilderness Preserve—(941) 338–3300, located on School Street, in Fort Myers Beach. More than forty acres of unspoiled live oak hammock and mangrove shoreline on Ester Bay. Watch birds, paint, or just relax.

Lover's Key State Park.

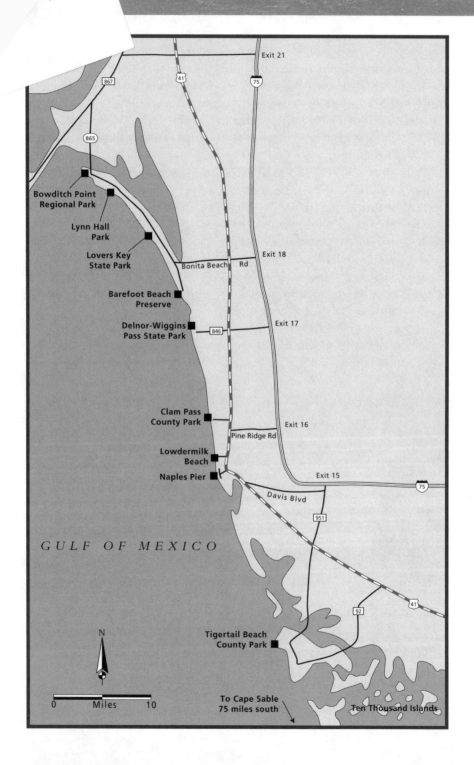

Exit 21

867

41

75

865

Bowditch Point
Regional Park

Lynn Hall
Park

Lovers Key
State Park

Exit 18

Bonita Beach   Rd

Barefoot Beach
Preserve

Delnor-Wiggins
Pass State Park

Exit 17

846

Clam Pass
County Park

Exit 16

Pine Ridge Rd

Lowdermilk
Beach

Naples Pier

Exit 15

75

Davis Blvd

951

GULF OF MEXICO

41

92

N

Tigertail Beach
County Park

0   Miles   10

To Cape Sable
75 miles south →

Ten Thousand Islands

Another one of the extremely remote beaches of the state, Cape Sable has more than 10 miles of beach on the sandy cape that makes up the southwest corner of mainland Florida (not shown on map). For someone with a few days to spend, though, it's as empty a piece of paradise as you can imagine. Accessible from Flamingo at the south end of Everglades National Park, it's a 10- to 20-mile kayak trip one-way and a relatively short trip by powerboat. Primitive camping is possible at three different locations along the cape; permits can be obtained at the visitor center at Flamingo.

For comfort's sake, this is a place best visited in winter due to the voracious mosquito and sand fly population in almost all of the national park. Adventurer Hugh Willoughby, the first white man to cross the Everglades, came across a dilapidated ship at Cape Sable with a desperate captain:

> He implored me to let him have a little sugar and coffee, as they were in an almost starving condition, the food having given out two weeks before; his men had been delayed in getting the lumber out, also by the mosquitoes that had infested the place where they were chopping to such an extent that one man nearly lost his life.

The pictures Willoughby took of Cape Sable in 1897 show a beach almost identical to today's. He wrote:

> We walked around the point along a very pretty sand beach, and watched the shark and tarpon that were occasionally rising to the surface. About a mile from where we were a large bunch of cocoanut-trees reached to the water's edge.

ACCESS: By boat or canoe/kayak from Flamingo at the south end of Everglades National Park. From US 1 in Florida City, take SR 9336 to the entrance to Everglades National Park, and stay on Main Park Road for 38 miles to Flamingo.

PARKING: Parking lots at Flamingo.

HOURS/FEES: Twenty-four hours; $10.00 entrance fee per vehicle for a seven-day pass, $5.00 for a powerboat, and $3.00 for a canoe or kayak; $20.00 yearly passes to the park.

AMENITIES: *Flamingo Visitor Center*—boat ramps, rest rooms, showers, canoe/kayak rentals, houseboat rentals, restaurant. *Cape Sable*—None.

ACTIVITIES: Beach walking, camping, playing Robinson Crusoe.

FOR MORE INFORMATION: Everglades National Park (941) 695–9145.

Ten Thousand Islands

There's a lot of Florida coast in this neck of the woods that you can't drive to, and the area known as Ten Thousand Islands continues the stretch of boat-only access. Popular with kayakers and boaters, the seemingly endless maze of islands has some beautiful beaches tucked away here and there. For the most part these are mangrove islands that hold little more than mosquitoes, but on a number of keys like Pavilion Key and Rabbit Key there are sand beaches. In addition, there are primitive camping areas with portable-toilets. Though it's an 8-mile paddle one-way, with some of it through the open waters of the Gulf, Pavilion Key is the longest beach and well worth the trip.

The mainland towns of Everglades City and Chokoloskee are the stepping-off points for trips through these islands, as well as the seven- to ten-day Wilderness Waterway kayak trip through Everglades National Park. The latter winds for 104 miles all the way down to Flamingo, and is a surprisingly popular—if at times grueling—trip. It has come to be what people associate with paddling the Everglades, though not a single part of the journey is in the Everglades itself. The "river of grass" that is the centerpiece of the national park is a maze that, to this day, few but the Seminole know how to navigate.

Chokoloskee was where the evil Mr. Watson, the historical figure in Peter Matthiessen's book *Killing Mr. Watson*, was killed when he refused to surrender and face charges regarding the workers who kept mysteriously disappearing on his plantation. Popular lore holds that the locals gunned him down like a vigilante squad, though in reality it seems he raised his shotgun first and it misfired. The islands are responsible for a number of fascinating characters; Loren "Totch" Brown's autobiography *Totch* is a good read to familiarize yourself with the place. Thousand Island salad dressing originated here, the name shortened from Ten Thousand Islands.

ACCESS: From US 41/Tamiami Trail, between Naples and Ochopee, turn south onto SR 29, go 3 miles to Everglades City, and another 3 miles to Chokoloskee. The Gulf Coast Visitor Center of the national park is on the south side of Everglades City.

PARKING: Free parking lot at the visitor center.

HOURS/FEES: Twenty-four hours; $10.00 entrance fee per vehicle for a seven day pass, plus $5.00 for a powerboat and $3.00 for a canoe or kayak; $20.00 yearly passes to the park. *Gulf Coast Visitor Center—* 9:00 A.M.–5:00 P.M., boat tours $13.00.

AMENITIES: *Gulf Coast Visitor Center—*Boat ramps, rest rooms, showers. *Pavilion Key, Rabbit Key, and Picnic Key—*Portable toilets.

ACTIVITIES: Canoeing, kayaking, boating, camping, beach walking, swatting mosquitoes.

FOR MORE INFORMATION: Everglades National Park (941) 695–3941.

Boat tours from visitor center (941) 695–4731.

Everglades City Chamber of Commerce (941) 695–3941.

Tigertail Beach County Park

Tigertail Beach offers the only decent access on all of Marco Island—a sprawling island community that has done its best to restrict the public. The county managed to carve out one beautiful niche for us, though. With full facilities and rentals available of everything imaginable, Tigertail is a great family place. Sailboarders can zip back and forth across the shallow bay between Sand Dollar Island and the beach, and the more leisurely can idle around in paddleboats and kayaks.

Behind the lagoon beach on Sand Dollar Island, there's a nice children's play area and Todd's at Tigertail Beachside Grill. Getting to the Gulf waters from the lagoon beach actually requires a lengthy walk to circumvent the lagoon. Still, once you're there you have all the room in the world to spread out.

ACCESS: From the east on US 41/Tamiami Trail, take CR 92/San Marco Road to Marco Island, turn right onto North Collier Avenue,

Tigertail Beach is a great family place.

go 0.8 mile to a left onto Kendall Drive, and go left on Hernando Drive to the park.

From I–75 or from Naples on US 41, take CR 951 south to Marco Island. It becomes North Collier Avenue on the island. Turn right onto Kendall Drive, then left onto Hernando Drive to the park.

PARKING: There are 190 parking spaces.

HOURS/FEES: 8:00 A.M.–sunset; $3.00 entrance fee per vehicle.

AMENITIES: Bathhouse, five boardwalks, rest rooms, showers, beach equipment rentals (sailboards, paddleboats, kayaks, sailboats, cabanas, beach chairs), food concession, handicapped beach wheelchair.

ACTIVITIES: Sunbathing, swimming, kayaking, sailing, paddleboating, sailboarding, bird-watching, volleyball.

FOR MORE INFORMATION: Tigertail Beach County Park (941) 642–8414.

Naples Pier

The Naples Pier is a venerable old structure that has weathered many a storm, and is the focal point of a long string of beautiful public beaches. There is street-end parking on most of the avenues, and the beach is equally nice all along. A popular fishing pier, it contains a bait shop and snack bar. Because it's open twenty-four hours, the wooden pier is also a favorite for romantic walks in the moonlight.

On the way to the beach, the Naples Visitor Center is conveniently located at the corner of 5th Avenue South and US 41, and you can pick up more information about Naples attractions. The downtown is a very chic, upscale area, and seems to be thriving. From a sleepy little town known for its swamp attractions, it's come a long way—it's now one of the nicest communities on the lower Gulf.

Naples Pier.

ACCESS: From US 41, turn west onto 5th Avenue south and go to Gulf Shore Boulevard, turn left and continue to 12th Avenue south.

PARKING: Metered street parking, lot parking.

HOURS/FEES: Twenty-four hours; 75 cents per hour.

AMENITIES: Historic pier, snack bar, bait shop, rest rooms, showers, picnic tables.

ACTIVITIES: Sunbathing, swimming, fishing, surfing, moonlit romance.

FOR MORE INFORMATION: Naples Pier (941) 434–4696.

Lowdermilk Beach

Another one of the Naples city beaches, Lowdermilk is one of the most popular in the area. Beach volleyball enthusiasts come here for the sand courts, and it generally draws a slightly younger crowd. Marriage ceremonies are not uncommon either, because the gazebo is the perfect place for those inclined toward beach weddings. There's a nice children's play area, and all the amenities of a major public beach. Though like most lower Gulf beaches it lacks lifeguards, the waters are calm and warm most of the year.

ACCESS: From US 41, take Banyan Boulevard west to the beach.

PARKING: Metered lot.

HOURS/FEES: 8:00 A.M.–11:00 P.M.; 75 cents per hour.

AMENITIES: Concession stand, sand volleyball courts, showers, children's play area, gazebos, pavilions, picnic tables, rest rooms.

ACTIVITIES: Volleyball, sunbathing, swimming, family picnics, getting married.

FOR MORE INFORMATION: Naples Community Services (941) 434–4687.

Clam Pass County Park

The county beach parks in Collier County are universally great places, and Clam Pass is perhaps the crown jewel. A long boardwalk runs through hundreds of acres of mangrove habitat, and regular tram service whisks you along back and forth to the beach. You're welcome to make the hike on foot, but make sure to wear shoes and realize that it's a long way. The boardwalk is constructed from recycled plastic planks, with an estimated 4,320,000 milk jugs having gone into the material.

Clam Pass County Park.

On the beach are the full concession services the county facilities offer, with kayaks, sailboards, and canoes, as well as umbrellas and chairs. There's also a snack bar. The beach is wide and luxuriously fine, with seemingly endless distances of it open to wandering. Just to the north is Clam Pass, a 25-yard-wide channel that's about 5 or 6 feet deep in the center. Many people wade or swim across to explore the secluded beach to the north.

ACCESS: From US 41 at the north end of Naples, take Seagate Road west to the beach.

PARKING: There are 182 metered spaces.

HOURS/FEES: 8:00 A.M.–sunset; $3.00 entrance fee per vehicle.

AMENITIES: Rest rooms, showers, picnic tables, beach equipment rental (kayaks, sailboards, canoes), food concession, handicapped beach wheelchair, boardwalk, tram.

ACTIVITIES: Swimming, sunbathing, nature viewing, kayaking, sailboarding, picnicking.

FOR MORE INFORMATION: Collier County Parks and Recreation (941) 353–0404.

Delnor-Wiggins Pass State Park

This stretch of coast north of Naples was acquired by the state in 1970 and passively managed as a wild area for its first two decades. In the past ten years, though, the local Supporters of Delnor-Wiggins Park have put in a lot of hard work to spruce it up. Restored boardwalks, a butterfly garden, and a conference center have all been completed. The volunteers have taken over a lot of the cleanup activities and small maintenance chores of the park, leaving the rangers free to do other tasks. It's a sprawling area of native habitat and the occasional Australian pine, interwoven with sandy pathways to the empty beaches. For those who treasure quietness, this is a lovely beach. In the interior is a boat ramp that gives access to the mangrove waterways, as well as an observation tower. Lifeguards patrol the beach in summer from 9:00 A.M.–5:00 P.M.

ACCESS: From US 41, take CR 846/Bluebill Avenue west to the beach.

From I–75, take exit 17 and go west for 5 miles.

PARKING: Five parking lots.

HOURS/FEES: 8:00 A.M.–sunset; $4.00 entrance fee per vehicle up to eight people, $2.00 if lone occupant, $1.00 walk-in or bike-in.

AMENITIES: Summer lifeguards, rest rooms, showers, picnic tables, boat ramp, observation tower, boardwalk.

ACTIVITIES: Swimming, fishing, picnicking, sunbathing, nature viewing, boating, hiking.

FOR MORE INFORMATION: Delnor-Wiggins Pass State Park (941) 597–6196.

Barefoot Beach Preserve

Though a little confusing to find, this beach is a marvel. Stretching all the way down to Wiggins Pass at the south end, the beach is part of 342 acres of barrier island open to the public. Beachcombers could not ask for a better stretch to spend the day strolling upon. The only off-putting part is that when you follow the signs and turn off Bonita Beach Road, you appear to be entering a gated community. Your first reaction is likely to think you made a wrong turn and turn around. If you approach the guardhouse, though, and stay in the right lane, you'll see a sign indicating that visitors to Barefoot Beach don't have to stop. This is one of the only cooperative examples I know of in all of Florida where a gated community has allowed access through its development to a public beach. Just pay attention to the 15-mile-per-hour speed limit and be patient with all the speed bumps.

The parking lot has a lovely butterfly garden adjacent to a thatched educational center where the Friends of Barefoot Beach meet. Guided canoe tours are offered at 9:00 A.M. each Sunday through the mangrove interior passages. The facilities are all very modern, and the emptiness of the place on most days is astonishing. With Delnor-Wiggins State Recreation Area occupying a long stretch on the other side of Wiggins Pass, this is one of largest areas of undeveloped wilderness beaches in the southern Gulf.

ACCESS: From US 41 (or exit 18 off I–75), take Bonita Beach Road west, turn left onto Lely Beach Road, and go 2 miles south.

Butterfly Garden at Barefoot Beach Preserve.

PARKING: You'll find 256 spaces.

HOURS/FEES: 8:00 A.M.–sunset; $3.00 entrance fee per vehicle.

AMENITIES: Visitor center, rest rooms, showers, picnic tables, boardwalk.

ACTIVITIES: Beach strolling, swimming, sunbathing, picnicking, nature viewing.

FOR MORE INFORMATION: Collier County Parks and Recreation (941) 353–0404.

Lovers Key State Park

Though most visitors to Lee County head for the spectacular sand and great shelling of Sanibel and Captiva, or go for the lively party atmosphere of Fort Myers Beach, those looking for wild and rugged beaches can find a unique atmosphere on Lovers Key. The entire key is a state park, with all manner of recreational opportunities—from kayaking to fishing to romance. A quarter-mile trip along a boardwalk, through mangroves and across shallow flats, takes you to the center beach. There actually isn't much beach here at all, though there are some fascinating, gnarled root structures from where erosion has hammered away at the shoreline.

To get to the nice beaches, you can take the tram to the southern end of the key, which is also where the Love Shack grill is located. There's also a good beach at the northern tip that you can access from parking just off the coast road and walking out along the edge of the pass. There are no facilities at this end, though. A concession inside the park entrance, and also on the bay side, rents kayaks and offers fishing charters to the bountiful waters of the surrounding area.

ACCESS: From US 41, head west on Bonita Beach Road to SR 865 North; it's 5 miles to Lovers Key, the entrance on your left.

From Fort Myers Beach, the key is 2 miles south on SR 865.

PARKING: Parking lots.

HOURS/FEES: 8:00 A.M.–sunset; $4.00 entrance fee per vehicle for up to eight people, $2.00 driver only, $1.00 walk-in or bike-in.

AMENITIES: Tram, rest rooms, pavilions, showers, picnic tables, walkways.

ACTIVITIES: Swimming, sunbathing, kayaking, fishing, beach walking, photography, nature viewing.

FOR MORE INFORMATION: Lovers Key State Park (941) 463–4588.

Lynn Hall Park aka Pelican Pier

Because it's the quickest beach to get to from the more densely populated inland areas of Fort Myers and Cape Coral, the strip on Fort Myers Beach around Pelican Pier is the most crowded and festive beach area in the region. Compared to the genteel beaches to the south and the old charm of Sanibel and Captiva, it's a wild hubbub of shops, restaurants, and activity. Most of the younger crowd comes to the beach here. The 560-foot pier is a good fishing or sight-seeing spot, stretching far out into the Gulf of Mexico. Though officially known as Lynn Hall Pier, it's known to the locals as Pelican Pier due to the ubiquitous presence of those long-beaked birds. Whether diving for fish on their own accord or trying to snatch a freebie from a fisherman, they line the pier in great numbers.

Off the pier there are all the usual amenities, including a new playground for children, covered picnic areas, and a nature kiosk with information about local plants, animals, and land formations. If you're heading on out to more remote locales, the main drag here is a good place to stock up on beach supplies as well as get some great seafood. The 25-cent LeeTran trolley runs from Bowditch Point past the pier and all the way south to Bonita Beach—definitely the best and cheapest way to get around.

ACCESS: From US 41, take SR 865/Gladiolus Drive west, then follow 865 south to Fort Myers Beach. The Fort Myers Beach Sky Bridge empties out to the parking area.

PARKING: Metered lots.

HOURS/FEES: Twenty-four hours, 365 days a year; 75 cents per hour.

AMENITIES: Playground, picnic shelters, rest rooms, showers, BBQ grills, fishing pier.

ACTIVITIES: Sunbathing, fishing, picnicking.

FOR MORE INFORMATION: Lee County Parks and Recreation (941) 463–1116.

Facility Supervisor, Paul Yacobelli yaccobp@leegov.com.

LeeTran trolley (941) 275–8726.

Bowditch Point Regional Park

When the crowds on the main strip of Fort Myers Beach get to be too much, cruise a half mile up the way to Bowditch Point. This is a pretty seventeen-acre park that takes up the northern tip of Fort Myers Beach. Parking is limited and involves obtaining a free permit from Lee County, but you can save yourself the hassle by just taking the 25-cent shuttle from Main Street Park. A long boardwalk stretches out to the beach from the bayside parking area, lined with cabbage palms. There are nice shaded picnic areas, and from the point you have a clear view of the Sanibel Lighthouse across the mouth of San Carlos Bay. Surrounded on three sides by water, it's a lovely stroll from the ocean beach around the point back to the parking area.

ACCESS: From US 41, take SR 865/Gladiolus Drive west, follow 865 south to Fort Myers Beach, turn right onto Estero Boulevard, and go 0.5 mile to the park.

From I–75, take exit 20, Daniels Road, west for 5 miles, then turn left onto CR 867/McGregor Boulevard south. After 2 miles make a soft left onto SR 865 south to Fort Myers Beach.

PARKING: Main Street Park at Fort Myers Beach, take free shuttle, or call Lee County Parks for a free on-site parking permit—sixty-eight spaces.

HOURS/FEES: Sunrise-sunset, free.

AMENITIES: Rest rooms, showers, picnic tables.

ACTIVITIES: Beach strolling, swimming, sunbathing, picnicking, nature viewing.

FOR MORE INFORMATION: Lee County Parks and Recreation (941) 463–1116.

LeeTran trolley (941) 275–8726.

The Sippi

While the beaches of Naples and Fort Myers are quite enough to occupy most of your time, what the area has traditionally been known for is the swamps of the wild interior. Lest this sound discouraging, they are swamps without peer. Ranging from the exotic orchids of the Fakahatchee Strand and Big Cypress—orchids that grow nowhere else in the world—to the teeming bird life of Corkscrew Swamp Sanctuary, these are special places. My aunt, Janet Reno, describes how she came to know the area:

> One afternoon when I was little we were sitting out in the front yard on Kendall Drive, which ended then just a half mile west at the edge of the Everglades. A mud-covered, rough-looking man walked into the yard. He had a funny way of talking and I was afraid of him, but Mother started talking with him and was immediately fascinated by him. He was Sippi Morris and through him we came to know our friends the Seminoles, and the magnificence and mystery of the Everglades.

I have sporadic memories of Sippi visits as a youth, which were always times of great excitement. You never knew when Sippi was going to show up, but you knew you were going to hear the best stories a person could tell. Sippi once got a murderer in the Dade County Jail to give him his breakfast. Sippi had been caught illegally hunting with the Dade County sheriff and volunteered to go to jail because someone had to rather than the sheriff. Sippi was covered in deer blood and told the murderer, "They say I killed three, but I only killed one."

Sippi drove his swamp buggy through every nook and cranny of the Faka-hatchee and Big Cypress and invented a number of items like the Sippi Super-Suction Snakebite System. This device attached to his windshield wipers and utilized suction cups to extract venom. He also was responsible for the Naples Swamp Buggy Race, a celebration of mud still taking place today. Though few of today's competitors know where the name came from, a section of deep water on the course is called "the sippi." The Miccosukee Indians treated Sippi like a slightly mad cousin and loved him dearly. There were few other white men who knew their land like he did, could wrestle alligators to sleep, and could install a glass eye on a 9-foot crocodile when it was required. Sippi was one of a kind.

Sanibel and Captiva Islands have become famous throughout the United States and elsewhere in the world for their beautiful barrier island beaches and enormous variety of seashells. There is a $3.00 toll to cross the causeway on to the islands. Ding Darling National Wildlife Refuge on Sanibel is a huge area of mangrove islands and waterways, popular with wildlife photographers and nature lovers. The bird life of Ding Darling is astounding. Inland, the city of Fort Myers is full of museums, theaters, and large performing arts venues like the Barbara B. Mann Hall.

The barrier island chain that includes Sanibel and Captiva stretches north and becomes disconnected from the road, so that North Captiva and Cayo Costa are accessible only by boat. The former is full of private homes, whereas the latter is a state park that offers one of the most extraordinary island experiences in Florida. Boca Grande Pass on the north end of Cayo Costa—famed tarpon fishing grounds—is the entrance to Charlotte Harbor, and splits up this region. The harbor extends for so far inland that you have to drive some 80 miles from Captiva in a large loop to come back out to the beach on the north side of Boca Grande, which is only 10 miles to the north as the crow flies.

Gasparilla Island State Park, littered with iguanas and exquisite beaches, takes up part of the community of Boca Grande, with the rest being a very wealthy community. There's more boat-only access to the north on Don Pedro Island, which has pristine beaches in a low-key state park. Up on Manasota Key, beaches become more easily accessible and the surroundings more proletarian. Englewood has happily developed at a snail's pace, a community straddling the Charlotte-Sarasota County line that neither county bothers to govern. Virtually all of the beaches of Manasota Key are expansive places with good facilities, and are the first beaches in the region to have lifeguards.

Access

From the south—Take exit 21 off I–75 west to Sanibel and Captiva.

From the north—Take exit 35 off I–75 south to SR 776 and Englewood.

Beaches

Bowman's Beach
Captiva Beach
Cayo Costa State Park
Gasparilla Island State Park
Don Pedro Island State Park
Stump Pass Beach State Park
Englewood Beach
Blind Pass Beach
Manasota Beach

Camping

Cayo Costa State Park—(941) 964–0375. Cayo Costa offers primitive camping for those wishing to set up tents. Visitors must carry in all food and drink; there are no facilities on the island. All items must be taken off the island upon departure. Cabins are available on Cayo Costa for $20 per night. Each cabin sleeps up to six people, and is furnished with three bunk beds and a table. The cabins are very primitive, with no electricity or any other amenities. They are centrally located to bathrooms and showers. There are grills available for cooking. Each cabin is conveniently located to the beach area and nature trails.

Fort Myers/Pine Island KOA—Reservations (800) 562–8505, (941) 283–2415, St. James City, Pine Island. An extensive campground with a store, laundry, and all facilities, 371 sites. Free bus trips to area beaches and attractions. Quiet natural setting, three ponds, free cable, wildlife, pool, and activities. Rates are $20–35 for a two-person tent site.

Myakka River State Park—(941) 361–6511. East of Venice. Two family campgrounds within walking distance from the Myakka River or the Upper Myakka Lake. Campsites accommodate tents, trailers, or motorized campers up to 35 feet long. Each site includes a picnic table and grill. Sites with water and electricity are available. A dump station for sewage disposal is also available. Rates are $11 May through November, $15 December through April. Six primitive campsites are located along a 39-mile hiking trail. Fees are $3.00 per person per night for adults. Children under eighteen are $2.00.

Other Points of Interest

Seminole Gulf Railway—(941) 275–8487, (800) 736–4853, Metro Mall Station in Fort Myers. Enjoy a nostalgic dinner, murder mystery, or sight-seeing excursion as you travel through southwestern Florida's subtropical terrain aboard an elegant, old-fashioned dining or coach excursion train. Call for locations and departure times.

Edison-Ford Winter Estates—(941) 334–3614, 2350 McGregor Boulevard, Fort Myers. Two of the area's most popular attractions are the homes of these famous next-door neighbors, Thomas Edison and Henry Ford. Tour Edison's botanical gardens, his laboratory, and the museum with the world's largest collection of Edison's inventions and memorabilia.

Calusa Nature Center and Planetarium—(941) 275–3435, 3450 Ortiz Avenue, Fort Myers. Offers a learning area for children, nature trails, an aviary, and a reproduction of a Seminole Indian village. Home to snakes, turtles, alligators, and crocodiles. Planetarium shows are presented twice daily.

Fort Myers Historical Museum—(941) 332–5955, 2300 Peck Street, Fort Myers. A restored depot with displays on Calusas and Seminole Indians, a scale model of turn-of-the-twentieth-century Fort Myers, and a restored railroad car from the 1930s.

Lee County Alliance of the Arts—(941) 939–2787, 10091 McGregor Boulevard, Fort Myers. A public art gallery featuring local craftsmen and artists. Recitals, concerts, and workshops.

Barbara B. Mann Performing Arts Hall and Gallery—(941) 481–4849, 8099 College Parkway, Fort Myers. The area's only full-sized and fully equipped stage for Broadway musicals, prominent entertainers, popular and classical music concerts on the campus of Edison Community College.

Boston Red Sox Spring Training—(941) 334–4700, located at the City of Palms Park, Fort Myers.

Broadway Palm Dinner Theatre—(941) 278–4422; (800) 475–7256, 1380 Colonial Boulevard, Fort Myers. Enjoy a lavish buffet then sit back and enjoy a Broadway-style live theatrical performance. Handicapped accessible.

Museum of the Islands—(941) 283–1525, 5728 Sesame Drive, Pine Island. Exhibitions on Pine Island pioneers, featuring artifacts from archaeological research on the island and a Calusa Indian dugout canoe. Admission fee.

Bailey-Matthews Shell Museum—(941) 395–2233, 3075 Sanibel/Captiva Road. Open 10:00 A.M.–4:00 P.M. Tuesday through Sunday; closed Monday. The Shell Museum is the only one of its kind in the United States. Exhibits are devoted to shells in art and history, shell habitats, rare specimens, fossil shells, and local Sanibel-Captiva shells. Museum members and children seven and under are free; youths eight to sixteen are $3.00; adults seventeen and up pay $5.00.

J. N. "Ding" Darling National Wildlife Refuge—(941) 472–1100, 1 Wildlife Drive, Sanibel Island. Open daily 9:00 A.M.–sunset; closed Friday. A wildlife photographer's paradise, this 5,000-acre sanctuary offers hiking, biking, and canoe trails. The 4-mile wildlife drive is $5.00 for cars, $1.00 for bikers and hikers. Narrated tram tours are $10.00 for adults, $5.00 for children. More than 200 species of birds nest here, many of them threatened or endangered. Alligators, turtles, river otters, armadillos, and other creatures may be spotted as well. Visitor center with guides and facilities. Also visit the Tarpon Bay Marina Center for canoe and kayak rentals, bike rentals, and independent or guided canoe and kayak tours around Tarpon Bay.

Sanibel Lighthouse Boardwalk—(941) 472–6477. The most frequently photographed feature of Sanibel Island, the lighthouse has been a landmark since 1884, when the entire island was a nature preserve. Visit the 400-foot, wheelchair-accessible boardwalk that leads visitors to the lighthouse.

The Useppa Museum—(941) 283–9600, Useppa Island, in the Pine Island National Wildlife Refuge. This museum tells the story of humans on Useppa Island for 11,000 years. The signature piece is a forensic restoration of the "Useppa Man" taken from a skeleton unearthed during an archeological dig in 1989. This island is accessible only by boat.

Manasota Beach.

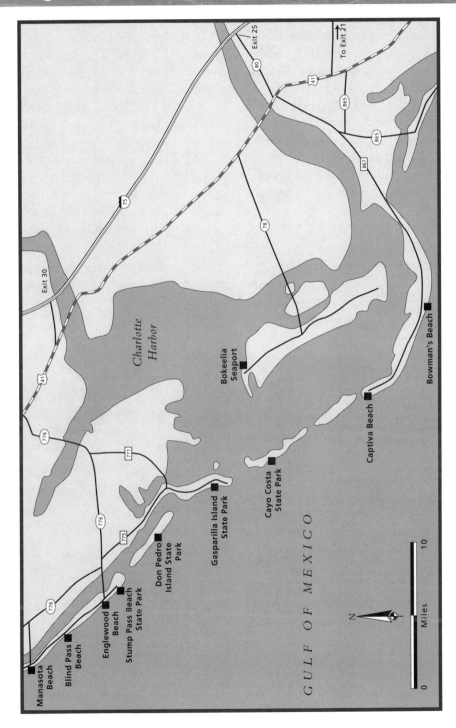

Manasota Beach

Blind Pass Beach

Englewood Beach

Stump Pass Beach State Park

Don Pedro Island State Park

Gasparilla Island State Park

Cayo Costa State Park

Bokeelia Seaport

Captiva Beach

Bowman's Beach

Charlotte Harbor

GULF OF MEXICO

Exit 30

Exit 25

Exit 21

To Exit 21

N

0   Miles   10

Bowman's Beach

Midway along Sanibel Island, this beach is a treasure. There's plenty of room to stretch out, comb the beach for shells, or have a picnic. The shelling on Sanibel is incomparable, since the east–west axis of the island allows for a greater variety to wash onto the beaches. Pets on leashes are welcome at Bowman's and the other Sanibel beaches, so the island has become popular with dog owners far and wide. On the bay side of Sanibel is Ding Darling National Wildlife Refuge, a favorite destination of nature lovers and wildlife photographers that takes up a full third of the island. The bird life here is tremendous, and it's a great place to explore by foot, boat, or kayak. Another nearby attraction is the Sanibel Lighthouse, which was built in 1884 and has a twin sister at Cape San Blas in the Panhandle. There's also a public beach at the lighthouse that wraps around the eastern tip of the island from bay to Gulf.

Collecting a crab trap.

ACCESS: From US 41, take SR 865/Gladiolus Drive west to CR 867, turn left, and go 7 miles south to Sanibel Island. Turn right onto Sanibel-Captiva Road and go north 5 miles to Bowman's Beach Road on your left.

From I–75, take exit 20, Daniels Road, west 5 miles to CR 867/ McGregor Boulevard. Turn left and go 10 miles south to Sanibel Island. Turn right onto Sanibel-Captiva Road and go north 5 miles to Bowman's Beach Road on your left.

PARKING: Metered lot.

HOURS/FEES: Sunrise–sunset; 75 cents per hour, $5.00 per day.

AMENITIES: Rest rooms, showers, grills.

ACTIVITIES: Shell collecting, swimming, sunbathing, picnicking, nature viewing, walking.

FOR MORE INFORMATION: Sanibel Island Parks (941) 472–4135.

Captiva Beach

At the north end of Captiva Island, this public beach is one of the seemingly forgotten parts of the barrier island chain. There is a little more commercial development on Captiva, and most of the people out here use the beaches in front of their resorts. The two public beaches of Captiva are not widely publicized, and remain retreats for those in the know. Unlike Sanibel, which has a variety of attractions beyond the beach, the main reason people come to Captiva is for the beautiful beaches—nothing more. The entire island has a great romantic reputation because of the seashells and tranquility, and attracts many couples on second honeymoons. Though at this writing Captiva Beach was still the only free beach on either island, the word is that it will soon have 75-cent-per-hour metered parking as well.

ACCESS: From I–75, take exit 20, Daniels Road west 5 miles to CR 867/McGregor Boulevard. Turn left and go 10 miles south to Sanibel Island, then turn right onto Sanibel-Captiva Road and go north 14 miles to a dead end. Beach access is on your left.

PARKING: Midsized lot.

HOURS/FEES: Sunrise–sunset; free.

AMENITIES: Rest rooms.

ACTIVITIES: Shell collecting, swimming, sunbathing, beach walking.

FOR MORE INFORMATION: Lee County Parks and Recreation (941) 338–3300.

Cayo Costa State Park

Lying on the south side of Boca Grande Pass—one of the most popular sport-fishing locations in the state for massive tarpon—is the pristine island of Cayo Costa. The entire island is a state park, and is disconnected from the roads of the Sanibel-Captiva chain. Cayo Costa is a tropical paradise, and while it's only a short boat ride from the mainland, it seems more like a deserted island of the South Pacific than somewhere in Florida. Famed Florida landscape photographer Clyde Butcher, who shoots in the large negative format of Ansel Adams, has chosen Cayo Costa as one of his few subjects outside the Everglades because of its unspoiled beauty.

All your supplies for a day trip or camping on the island need to be packed in and packed out. The island is not entirely without amenities, though. Inexpensive, primitive cabins can be rented for only $20 a night. In the interior of Cayo Costa are acres of pine forests, along with hammocks of oak and palm. Mangroves fringe the bayside. If you want to get well and truly lost in wild seclusion, this is definitely the place.

ACCESS: From US 41 in North Fort Myers, head west on SR 78/Pine Island Road to Pine Island; turn right (north) and continue 6 miles to Bokeelia Island Seaport Pier.

PARKING: Ferry parking lot.

HOURS/FEES: 8:00 A.M.–sunset; $2.00 entrance fee, 50 cents for bay-beach tram ride.

AMENITIES: Rest rooms, picnic tables, showers, cabins, hiking trails.

ACTIVITIES: Hiking, paddling, snorkeling, shell collecting, camping, swimming, sunbathing.

FOR MORE INFORMATION: Cayo Costa State Park (941) 964–0375.

Ferry service: Captiva Cruises (941) 472–5300.

Jugcreek Marina (941) 283–9512.

Tropic Star of Pine Island (941) 283–0015.

Gasparilla Island State Park

Visiting Gasparilla Island and the community of Boca Grande mirrors somewhat the experience of driving through the exclusive community of Jupiter Island directly across the state. Unlike there, however, Boca Grande has tried to actively discourage local usage of Gasparilla Island by charging a hefty $3.50 toll simply to gain access to the island. This is offset somewhat by the state park system only charging $2.00 for usage of the state park beaches, which are absolutely worth the expense of getting there. At the south end of the island is the historic lighthouse, which sits on the edge of Boca Grande Pass. Looking across to the south you can see Cayo Costa. Boats drift through the pass with the strong currents, hoping to hook into a large tarpon or other fish.

On shore, iguanas surprise you with their ubiquitous presence, scrambling across sand dunes and sunning themselves in people's yards. From pets gone wild, they've reproduced in extraordinary numbers on the south end of the island. While the lighthouse and the pass are must-sees, the currents are far too treacherous for swimming and the beach is limited in length, with the remains of a concrete fishing pier delineating the north end. The best beaches are a half mile to the north, in Parking Area 2 and beyond. These beaches are stunning and rarely crowded, though caution should still be used regarding the currents. A bike path runs much of the length of the island, and there is some beautiful and lavish architecture worth admiring at a slow pace.

ACCESS: From US 41, take SR 776 west 5 miles to CR 771, turn left and go south 8 miles to CR 775, then cross the toll bridge at Boca Grande Causeway to Gasparilla Island. It's 7 miles south to the bottom of island.

From I–75, take exit 34 and head south on CR 777 to CR 775 to the Boca Grande Causeway.

PARKING: Parking lot.

HOURS/FEES: 8:00 A.M.–sunset; $2.00 entrance fee.

AMENITIES: Lighthouse, visitor center, rest rooms, picnic tables, pavilion, grills.

ACTIVITIES: Shell collecting, fishing, picnicking, swimming, sunbathing.

FOR MORE INFORMATION: Gasparilla Island State Park (941) 964–0375.

Don Pedro Island State Park

This park occupies 129 acres of a barrier island lying across the Intracoastal Waterway from Cape Haze, just to the north of Gasparilla Island and Boca Grande. A typical combination of bayside mangroves and beautiful beach, the beach extends for a mile of powdery white sand. Because the toll to Boca Grande is so hefty, many locals looking for their own bit of secluded paradise run their boats out to Don Pedro. There are docks on the bay side, accessed via a channel from the Intracoastal Waterway south of the Cape Haze power-line crossing. The channel depth is only 2.5 feet, so caution and idle speed are necessary.

Though there are rest rooms, you need to bring your own drinking water and other supplies. While it's referred to as an island of its own, it's actually a part of a large barrier island that has private home ownership at the north and south end. A barge runs out to the island for residents who want to carry cars on and off, but costs $50 a trip. The residents would rather the island have no visitors, but the state facilities allow visitors access to the beaches of the entire island. If you can get public access to a beach in Florida, you can walk to your heart's content, because all beach below the mean high-tide line is public.

ACCESS: By private boat or kayak.

PARKING: Docks.

HOURS/FEES: 8:00 A.M.–sunset; $2.00 entrance fee.

AMENITIES: Docks, rest rooms, picnic tables, pavilion, grills.

ACTIVITIES: Shell collecting, boating, picnicking, swimming, sunbathing.

FOR MORE INFORMATION: Don Pedro Island State Park (941) 964–0375.

Stump Pass Beach State Park

What's remarkable about the southern Gulf Coast is that so many of the public beaches seem to stretch on forever. Stump Pass Beach is a textbook case, located at the end of the road south of Englewood Beach. For those lucky enough to find a parking spot—nigh impossible on weekends—there's a wonderful beach that drifts far off to the south to Stump Pass. The pass itself has been the subject of local controversy, because boaters want it continuously dredged for access to the Gulf, and the pass obstinately persists in shoaling up at a rapid rate. Left to its own devices, the pass can disappear completely with one major storm. Some locals are also grumpy about the state owning the beach now. Not so long ago it was a free facility with roadside parking, and no posted hours indicating that it was open.

Stump Pass Beach.

Judging by the number of visitors still, most people are fine with the new setup, and the state does a good job with facilities and natural preservation. With Englewood Beach to the north just having completed a massive over-haul, some of the crowds at Stump Pass should dwindle a bit.

ACCESS: From US 41, take SR 776 west 12 miles to Beach Road, turn left onto Englewood Beach, then left again (south) to the park entrance.

From I–75, take exit 34 and head south on CR 777 to SR 776 south to Beach Road.

PARKING: Forty to fifty spaces.

HOURS/FEES: 8:00 A.M.–sunset; $2.00 entrance fee, $1.00 walk-in or bike-in.

AMENITIES: Rest rooms, picnic tables, boardwalks.

ACTIVITIES: Beach walking, shell collecting, picnicking, swimming, sunbathing.

FOR MORE INFORMATION: Stump Pass Beach State Park (941) 964–0375.

Englewood Beach

The major public beach for the Englewood area, located on the lower half of the picturesque and lightly developed Manasota Key, has been completely renovated. The new beach facilities include brick walkways, elevated rest rooms, sand volleyball courts, and landscaping. Eventually a basketball court will be built across the street. Because Englewood is the only Gulf beach that Charlotte County has, they've put a lot of money into making the beach as attractive as possible. If Englewood's northern neighbor, Venice, seems like a low-key community, then Englewood has developed it to an even finer art. Straddling the Charlotte/Sarasota county line, the residents pride them-selves on their ability to run their own lives without much governing by either county. The eastern edge of town disappears into countless square miles of state forest, and the Myakka River to the northeast is a beautiful canoeing area.

ACCESS: From US 41, take SR 776 west 12 miles to Beach Road and turn left to Englewood Beach.

From I–75, take exit 34, head south on CR 777 to SR 776 south to Beach Road.

PARKING: One hundred-plus spaces.

HOURS/FEES: 6:00 A.M.–11:00 P.M.; free.

AMENITIES: Rest rooms, showers, picnic tables, pavilions, boardwalks, volleyball courts.

ACTIVITIES: Volleyball, picnicking, swimming, sunbathing.

FOR MORE INFORMATION: Charlotte County Parks (941) 627–1628.

Blind Pass Beach

Manasota Key is one of the best examples of low-key development in this area, and the drive along the coastal road is a peaceful experience. Many of the homes have maintained the native vegetation, and are hidden among dense stands of oaks, sea grape, mastic, and other trees. A shady canopy extends over the road for stretches. Midway up the key is Blind Pass Beach, with more than a half mile of beachfront and almost unlimited parking. The Hermitage, one of the oldest structures in Englewood, sits on the beach at the southern end of the property. Right now it is in the midst of renovation as a facility for artists.

The beach is expansive, and rarely too crowded. The roads that empty onto the key from the mainland, at Englewood Beach and Manasota Beach, absorb the bulk of area beachgoers. The only odd thing about the facilities is the location of the children's play area—far to the rear of the parking area on the other side of the road, in a desolate place. Judging by the number of kids enjoying themselves in the water and on the beach, though, no one seems to mind.

ACCESS: From the south on US 41, take SR 776 west 12 miles to Beach Road, turn left to Englewood Beach, turn right onto Manasota Key Road, and go 3 miles north.

From the north on US 41, take CR 775/Englewood Road south from Venice for 3 miles, turn right onto Manasota Beach Road, and go west to Manasota Beach. Turn left onto Manasota Key Road and continue south for 1.5 miles.

PARKING: Free lot.

HOURS/FEES: 6:00 A.M.–midnight; free.

AMENITIES: Rest rooms, showers, picnic shelter, nature trail, canoe launch.

ACTIVITIES: Swimming, sunbathing, picnicking, fishing, canoeing.

FOR MORE INFORMATION: Sarasota County Parks (941) 316–1172. Shelter rental information (941) 474–8919.

Blind Pass Beach is rarely crowded.

Manasota Beach is a wide and daunting stretch of sand to cross on a scorching summer day. It's one of the first places coming up from the south where you find year-round lifeguards, perched high up in a state-of-the-art tower building that gives them a panoramic view of the coast. Though the beach is nominally less than a quarter mile in length, the miles of beach that stretch off in either direction, with nary a condo or obtrusive building in sight, are open for strolling. In fact, if you walked 3 or 4 miles to the north, you would find yourself at Caspersen Beach in Venice. There are lots of picnic shelters and a pavilion, and weekends see plenty of families out enjoying festive lunches. On the bay side is a boat ramp for access to the waterway, though it's a long run to the north to Venice Inlet or to one of the passes to the south to get out into the ocean. The 620-foot boardwalk that starts at the boat ramp extends as a nature trail through the mangroves.

ACCESS: From US 41, go south on CR 775 from Venice for 3 miles, turn right onto Manasota Beach Road, and go west to the beach.

PARKING: Parking lots.

HOURS/FEES: 6:00 A.M.–midnight; free.

AMENITIES: Lifeguards, boat ramp, docks, rest rooms, showers, picnic shelter.

ACTIVITIES: Swimming, sunbathing, picnicking, fishing, boating, shell collecting.

FOR MORE INFORMATION: Sarasota County Parks (941) 316–1172.

Shelter rental information (941) 474–8919.

Shelling

The pursuit of seashells has long been one of the greatest joys of beach wandering. Because the shelled creatures that make a home in the sea are so rich and varied, you can always depend on new and extraordinary finds no matter how long you do it. Shells are an artistic pleasure in their intricacy, in the perfection of nature's design. Everyone has different tastes in art, so everyone has different tastes in shells. One person may be taken by miniatures, another by conchs. Whether you're five or seventy-five, there's the same delight in finding a shell that truly strikes your fancy. By the time my brother was ten, he had filled his shelves with a stunning collection.

The islands of Sanibel and Captiva are known throughout the United States as having some of the finest shelling beaches in the country. Avid shellers will be out at dawn scouring the beach for new gems, or prowling the beach after a storm to see what has turned up. In fact, the posture that legions of shell hunters conduct their forays in has been given a name: the "Sanibel Stoop." Gulf hurricanes move such huge quantities of sand around that the beaches are turned upside down. The pass between Sanibel and Captiva was completely filled up with sand by one storm, and now the two islands are connected. While the taking of live shells is prohibited, virtually everything you find out of the water on the beach is going to be empty housing. The area is home to the only shell museum in the country, indicating just how serious folks are about their shells in these parts.

The Venice beaches are some of the prettiest in the lower Gulf, especially south of the Venice Inlet where there are still rolling dunes and long expanses of undeveloped beach like Caspersen Beach. Like most of the communities of southern Sarasota County, Venice rolls along relatively unchanged and its own slow place. The coastline around Venice has largely been protected from development, and there are no "pink monsters" among the modest homes. North Jetty Park is still the same great fishing and surfing hangout it was twenty years ago.

Sarasota is an honest-to-goodness city these days, home of the prestigious New College, the Ringling Museum of Art, and many other cultural attractions. The Mote Marine Aquarium, one of the highlights of Sarasota, is the most advanced marine research facility in the state, and has a fantastic shark tank and other displays. The beaches are considerably more bustling with people and energy than elsewhere, with Siesta Key Beach being party central.

Jogging back inland to downtown and out again to the beaches of Lido Key, the social scene drops off a notch, and North Lido finds you in relative seclusion. Public beach access disappears completely throughout the entire length of Longboat Key, but is thankfully restored on the Bradenton beaches on Anna Maria Island. Seven and a half miles of funky old Florida, there are no fast-food restaurants and no major hotels on the entire island. It's just old seaside inns and cottages, with Australian pines and dirt parking lots at the beaches. The area was developed in the early 1900s by the "father of the Fig Newton," Charles Roser.

Access

From the south—Exit 35 off I–7, west to Venice.

From the north—Exit 1 off I–275, south on US 41 to Bradenton.

Beaches

Caspersen Beach

Venice Pier/Brohard Park

North Jetty Beach

Turtle Beach/Palmer Point Beach

Siesta Key Beach Park

Lido Beach/North Lido Beach

Coquina Beach/Cortez Beach

Manatee Beach

Egmont Key State Park

Camping

Myakka River State Park—(941) 361–6511, east of Venice. Two family campgrounds within walking distance from the Myakka River or Upper Myakka Lake. Campsites accommodate tents, trailers, or motorized campers up to 35 feet long. Each site includes a picnic table and grill. Sites with water and electric are available. A dump station for sewage disposal is also available. Rates are $11 May through November, $15 December through April. Six primitive campsites are located along a 39-mile hiking trail: $3.00 per person per night for adults; children under eighteen are $2.00.

Oscar Scherer State Park—(941) 483–5956, on US 41 north of Venice. Pineland woods not far from the coast. Full-facility camping with RV hookups. Base rates June through October run $11, November through May $15. Rates are per night, per site, for up to four persons. It's $2.00 more for electric.

Gulf Beach Campground—(941) 349–3839, near Turtle Beach just below Sarasota. Most lots are heavily shaded, and the farthest you can be from the water is 700 feet. All lots have full hookups with up to fifty-amp service and cable TV. Phone service is available. All lots are available as tent sites. Showers, Laundromat, and pay phones. Rates from April 22 through December 21 are $19–31; from December 21 through April 21, $29–39.

Frog Creek Campground and RV Park—(800) 771–FROG (3764), www. frogcreekrv.com, 8515 Bayshore Road, Palmetto, near the foot of the Sunshine Skyway Bridge. Sites under shady oak trees; tents and pop-up trailers welcome; new laundry and bathhouse; full hookups. Rates are $22 per night, $135 per week; $18 per night for wilderness sites, and a Web-site special of seven nights for $100.

Other Points of Interest

Mote Marine Aquarium—(800) 691–MOTE, (941) 388–2451, 1600 Ken Thompson Parkway on City Island, just south of Longboat Key. Open 10:00

A.M.–5:00 P.M. daily. Part of the Mote Marine Laboratory, the foremost marine research facility in the state. Come face to face with your fears in the 135,000-gallon shark tank. Visit with resident manatees Hugh and Buffett and meet endangered sea turtles in the aquarium's newest exhibits. Reach out and hold a stingray, a sea urchin, or even a horseshoe crab in a 30-foot touch tank.

De Soto National Memorial—(941) 792–0458, on the south edge of Tampa Bay in Bradenton. Commemorates De Soto's 1539 landing and his four-year journey through the United States. During the summer, park rangers in sixteenth-century dress reenact the times. Nature trail and visitor center.

Oscar Scherer State Park—(941) 483–5956, on US 41 north of Venice. A 1,384-acre pine and scrub woodland. There are streams for canoeing, a swimming lake, fresh- and saltwater fishing, campgrounds, nature trails, bicycle paths, a recreation hall, and picnic areas. The park is 5 miles north of Venice and 2 miles south of Osprey.

Ringling Museum of Art—(941) 359–5700, (941) 351–1660, 5401 Bay Shore Road, Sarasota. Walk around the lushly landscaped grounds where circus magnate John Ringling and his wife Mable lived in the 1920s, and through the thirty-room Ringling winter residence built on the waters of Sarasota Bay. The Art Museum, housed in a pink Italian Renaissance villa, contains more than 500 years of European, American and world art. Experience life under the "big top" in the Museum of the Circus, where circus memorabilia is on display.

Marie Selby Botanical Gardens—(941) 366–5731, 811 South Palm Avenue, Sarasota. Nine-acre botanical gardens overlooking Sarasota Bay. A display greenhouse replicates a mini rain forest, showcasing orchids, colorful bromeliads, and other unusual tropical plants.

Myakka River State Park and Wilderness Preserve—(941) 365–0100, on SR 72, 9 miles east of I–75. Florida's largest park, covering more than 29,000 acres of wetlands, prairies and dense woodlands along the twisting Myakka River and Upper Myakka Lake. For a close-up view, take a boat or tram ride leaving from the boat basin. There are numerous nature trails in Myakka River State Park, as well as a small natural history museum and a bird walk. You can also camp, fish, boat, bicycle, and hike here. Open 8:00 A.M.–sunset.

Warm Mineral Springs—(941) 426–1692, 12200 San Servando Avenue, east of Venice off US 41. This natural spring is a focal watering place and spa of world renown forming a 2.5-acre lake and some 9 million gallons of water per day. The temperature of the lake holds at a year-round eighty-seven degrees Fahrenheit.

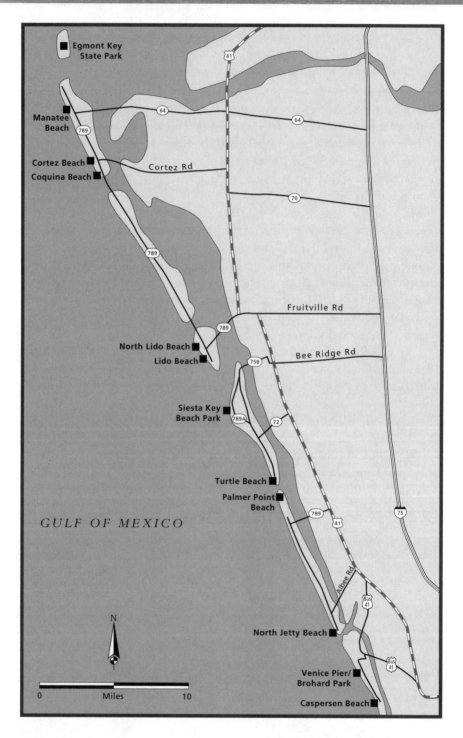

Egmont Key
State Park

41

64

64

Manatee
Beach
789

Cortez Rd

Cortez Beach
Coquina Beach

70

789

Fruitville Rd

789

Bee Ridge Rd

North Lido Beach
Lido Beach
758

Siesta Key
Beach Park
789A   72

Turtle Beach

Palmer Point
Beach
789
41

GULF OF MEXICO

75

Albee Rd

Bus
41

North Jetty Beach

Bus
41

Venice Pier/
Brohard Park

Caspersen Beach

N

0   Miles   10

☆☆☆

Down at the south end of Venice, where Harbor Drive dead-ends, is a beach that seems out of place in this part of the Gulf. The dune structures are still intact, and the road runs like a tunnel through them at one point, with sand constantly cascading out into the roadway. It's more reminiscent of the Outer Banks of North Carolina or a few barrier islands of Florida's Atlantic coast. The parking areas are expansive, and an 1,100-foot-long boardwalk connects them all. The beachfront that's within Caspersen Park runs for nearly 2 glorious miles of Manasota Key, most of it in its natural, wild state.

It's rarely crowded, even on weekends, because Venice has so many public beaches and Caspersen is out toward the margins. This is one of the best shelling beaches in the area, as well as fertile grounds for fossilized shark's teeth. There aren't lifeguards or much for the young to do here, but for lovers of beach walking and seclusion, this is a breathtaking stretch of sand.

ACCESS: Coming from the north or south into Venice on US 41, fork off onto US 41 Business, turn west onto Avenida del Circo, turn right onto Airport Avenue, go 1 mile to Harbor Drive south, and turn left. Follow this road 2 miles to its end.

PARKING: Parking lots.

HOURS/FEES: 6:00 A.M.–midnight; free.

AMENITIES: An 1,100-foot boardwalk, nature trails, picnic area, rest rooms, showers.

ACTIVITIES: Prehistoric shark's tooth collecting, hiking, swimming, sunbathing, picnicking.

FOR MORE INFORMATION: Sarasota County Parks (941) 316–1172.

Venice Pier/Brohard Park

The Venice Pier is part of the larger Brohard Beach, adjacent to the Venice Airport. Jutting out 740 feet into the ocean, the venerable old pier is one of the cheaper ocean fishing piers you can find—it's only a buck for entrance. Framing the entrance to the pier is Sharky's Restaurant, a quite good seafood venue with an outdoor deck. Their frozen piña coladas and daiquiris are just the thing for enjoying under an umbrella on a broiling summer day in the upper nineties. Children love doing somersaults down the berms of the beach and then running into the water to rinse off before doing it all over again.

The beach stretches off a long way to the south, with another parking area called South Brohard Park, and for all practical purposes it's one big public beach between the pier and Caspersen Beach. At the south entrance

Venice Fishing Pier.

to Brohard, there's a special dog park where owners can let their animals play with each other unleashed. Fourth of July sees a big fireworks display off the pier; the Sharks Tooth Festival in September is another popular event.

ACCESS: Coming from the north or south into Venice on US 41, fork off onto US 41 Business, turn west onto Avenida del Circo, turn right onto Airport Avenue, go 1 mile to Harbor Drive South, and turn left. The pier is within 0.5 mile on your right.

PARKING: Parking lots.

HOURS/FEES: Beach—6:00 A.M.–midnight; free.

Pier—6:00 A.M.–sunset; $1.00 for adults, 50 cents for children under 12.

AMENITIES: Fishing pier, restaurant, picnic area, rest rooms, showers, bait shop.

ACTIVITIES: Swimming, sunbathing, dining, fishing.

FOR MORE INFORMATION: Sarasota County Parks (941) 316–1172.

North Jetty Beach

Over the years, North Jetty Beach in Venice has changed little. It's the quintessential Florida surfer's beach, a sprawling dirt parking lot littered with Australian pines. At the edge of the inlet sits an old bait and tackle shop and restaurant called North Jetty Fish Camp. When hurricanes or winter storms pump waves in, surfers flock here from miles around to ride the nice waves that peel off the jetty.

The jetty is also an attraction for local fishermen, and is one of the best fishing spots in Venice. Picnic tables and grills are scattered throughout the park, along with volleyball and horseshoe courts. What with all the recreation—and lifeguards, too—it's one of the best family outing beaches in the area. The beach is extremely wide near the jetty, and if you walk north for about a half mile you arrive at another public beach, Nokomis Beach, with full facilities as well.

ACCESS: From US 41 on the north side of Venice, take Albee Road west. Turn left onto Casey Key Road and go south to the end.

PARKING: Parking lots.

HOURS/FEES: 6:00 A.M.–midnight; free.

AMENITIES: Lifeguards, rest rooms, showers, bait shop, picnic shelters, horseshoe courts, volleyball courts, food concession.

ACTIVITIES: Surfing, swimming, volleyball, horseshoes, fishing, picnicking.

FOR MORE INFORMATION: Sarasota County Parks (941) 316–1172.

Mote Marine Laboratory and Aquarium (800) 691–MOTE.

Turtle Beach/Palmer Point Beach

Like North Jetty, this is another popular family beach. There's plenty of parking and 1,200 feet of beachfront, with volleyball courts and a playground. It's a favorite put-in spot for area boaters, with two boat ramps on the Intracoastal Waterway. Unfortunately, the closing of Midnight Pass a short distance to the south has created a long run to the Gulf. On the plus side, the closing of the pass in 1984 has allowed access to a wonderful secluded beach that was previously accessible only by boat. Palmer Point Beach is located on both the southern tip of Siesta Key and the northern end of Casey Key, and can be accessed on Siesta Key from Turtle Beach. There is development in between, but you can walk along the water's edge around the rocks that line these units, and reach undeveloped wild beach after a mile or so. Palmer Point Beach is the old home of Mote Marine Laboratory, now located closer to Sarasota.

> **ACCESS:** From US 41, take Stickney Point Road/SR 72 west to Siesta Key, turn left onto Midnight Pass Road, and continue 2.5 miles south to Turtle Beach.
>
> From I–75, take exit 36 to SR 72/Clark Road and drive west to Siesta Key.

PARKING: Parking lot at Turtle Beach.

HOURS/FEES: 6:00 A.M.–midnight; free.

AMENITIES: Rest rooms, showers, building for meetings, boat ramps, picnic shelters, horseshoe courts, volleyball court, playground equipment.

ACTIVITIES: Boating, sunbathing, swimming, volleyball, horseshoes, fishing, picnicking, beach walking.

FOR MORE INFORMATION: Sarasota County Parks (941) 316–1172.

Mote Marine Laboratory and Aquarium (800) 691–MOTE.

Turtle Beach.

The lower Gulf is known as a retirement area, so young people occasionally get exasperated with the lack of fellow youngsters at area beaches. For the young, and the young at heart, Siesta Key Beach is a mecca. It is *the* party beach of the lower Gulf, with people coming from dozens of miles away to enjoy it. There's nothing quite like it anywhere else around, and it's a bit of a shock to the system compared to the relatively sedate beaches to the north or south.

Despite the enormous parking area, cars still line up on weekends jockeying for spots. A beach shuttle runs from downtown Sarasota, which is a good way to avoid the parking hassle. Out on the beach, intense games of beach volleyball take place on the ten courts. This is not the place for friendly family games, but more a proving ground in fierce two-on-two competition. The rest of the beach is a little more mellow, an incredibly wide expanse of fine white sand that comfortably hosts thousands of people. The shallow waters are good for swimming, and lifeguards keep an eye on everyone.

Volleyball on Siesta Key Beach.

There's a large concession area to get some food and drink in the shade when the sun gets to be too much. Away from the beach, there are also tennis courts, a ball field, and soccer field. It's definitely a one-stop recreation area, which is part of why it's so incredibly popular. This is the only place on the Gulf where an 800-space parking lot is referred to on the county Web site as "limited parking."

ACCESS: From US 41, take Stickney Point Road/SR 72 west to Siesta Key, turn right onto Midnight Pass Road, go 1.5 miles to Beach Road, fork left, and continue 0.5 mile to the parking area.

From I–75, from exit 36, take SR 72/Clark Road west to Siesta Key.

PARKING: 800 spaces, thirteen more beach accesses along Beach Road with limited parking.

HOURS/FEES: 6:00 A.M.–midnight; free.

AMENITIES: Lifeguards, rest rooms, showers, food concessions, picnic shelters, pavilion, tennis courts, ball field, volleyball courts, soccer field, twenty-station fitness trail, playground equipment, beach wheelchairs.

ACTIVITIES: Swimming, sunbathing, soccer, volleyball, baseball, tennis, working out, picnicking.

FOR MORE INFORMATION: Sarasota County Parks (941) 316–1172.

Lifeguard station, Siesta Key Beach.

Lido Beach/North Lido Beach

The Lido beaches are a yin and yang of popular bustle and quieter passive recreation. The main beach, Lido Beach, has been one of the area favorites since 1926 when John Ringling—of the Ringling Brothers Circus—and other businessmen built a pavilion, dock, and bathhouses out here. Sarasota has always been heavily identified with Ringling, who left a legacy not only of the circus but also of a prestigious art college. In 1940, a depression-era Works Progress Administration project built the Lido Beach Casino, a grand structure that combined features of Frank Lloyd Wright, art deco, and modern architecture into a popular tourist attraction. The building was demolished in 1969 before renovation could be done, and has been replaced by a modern structure. Lido has a heated indoor swimming pool, a gift shop, and 3,100 feet of beachfront to handle many of the Sarasotans who don't go to Siesta Key. It's another lifeguarded beach, and a good family spot.

For those looking for a bit more quiet, North Lido Beach is less than a mile to the north with far fewer facilities, but it has an equal amount of beachfront to its southern counterpart. There are no lifeguards on duty, and parking is a lot more limited. North Lido is undeveloped beyond a nature trail, and is ideal if all you want is sand, sun, and seclusion.

ACCESS: From US 41, head west on Fruitville Road to SR 789/John Ringling Causeway. Continue through St. Armand's Circle and 0.5 mile along Ben Franklin Drive to the beach.

From I–75, take exit 37 onto SR 780/Fruitville Road and go west to the John Ringling Causeway.

PARKING: Four hundred parking spaces, limited parking at North Lido.

HOURS/FEES: 6:00 A.M.–midnight; free.

AMENITIES: Lifeguards, rest rooms, showers, food concessions, gift shop, playground equipment, heated swimming pool with diving board, wheelchair-accessible observation decks, beach wheelchairs.

ACTIVITIES: Swimming (pool and ocean), sunbathing, picnicking, children's play.

FOR MORE INFORMATION: Sarasota County Parks (941) 316–1172.

Coquina Beach/Cortez Beach

The southern beaches of Anna Maria Island are a step back in time in Florida. Australian pines line long, rambling dirt parking areas, and facilities are relatively minimal. Cortez Beach is marked by three old concrete jetties that are closed to the public, but help shape the waves for surfers who call the popular surf spot "Grandpa's Wharves." The beach is a bit narrower here than to the south at Coquina Beach, but it's still quite nice. When the surf is flat—which is most of the time—the areas between the jetties are great swimming spots.

Just south of the last of the jetties, Coquina Beach begins and goes on for a bountiful mile. The beach is wide, white sand, with year-round lifeguards and beach volleyball courts. The Patio Café serves up standard lunches and snacks. Across the road is a playground and boardwalk that leads out to the Intracoastal Waterway. Because Coquina and Cortez are separated from Sarasota by the long expanse of Longboat Key and there's not much population directly inland, they rarely see crowds.

ACCESS: From US 41, drive west on Cortez Road for 8 miles. Cross over the drawbridge and turn left at the traffic light onto Gulf Drive. Cortez Beach is the first open parking area on your right, and Coquina Beach is just past Cortez Beach, also on the right.

From I–75, take exit 41 and go west on SR 70 for 11.5 miles. Turn left (west) onto Cortez Road, cross over the drawbridge, and turn left at the traffic light.

PARKING: Parking lots.

HOURS/FEES: Sunrise–sunset; free.

AMENITIES: Lifeguards 9:00 A.M.–5:00 P.M. (except 9:00 A.M.–7:00 P.M. during Daylight Saving Time) rest rooms, volleyball courts, showers, food concessions, covered pavilion, nature walk.

ACTIVITIES: Surfing, fishing, swimming, volleyball, sunbathing, picnicking.

FOR MORE INFORMATION: Manatee County Parks (941) 742–5923.

Manatee Beach

What Manatee Beach is most famous for is one of the best breakfast spots on the Gulf Coast, the unpreposessing Café on the Beach. The all-you-can-eat pancake breakfast for $3.50 is a popular favorite, as are the tasty Belgian waffles with strawberries. Sitting back with a cup of coffee and a full belly, gazing across the patio at the broad beach as the sun lights up the Gulf in the morning, is one of life's simpler pleasures. The beach is so wide that it seems like an infinite playground, and there's a small and relatively new concrete fishing pier that juts into the Gulf. Being right at the end of the Palma Sola Causeway, which leads out from the communities on the south side of Tampa Bay, it's a popular young people's beach.

The community around Manatee Beach is part of its charm, because it has resisted development and remained a low-key blend of one- and two-

Café on the Beach, Manatee.

story motels, cottages, and houses. It's a great place to look for quiet and inexpensive vacation rentals, not too far from all the attractions of Tampa Bay.

ACCESS: From US 41, go west on SR 64/Manatee Avenue for 8 miles. Cross Palma Sola Causeway to the beach.

From I–75, take exit 42, and go west on SR 64 for 12 miles to the beach.

PARKING: Parking lot at Manatee Beach (40th Street), street-end access between 28th and 72nd Street.

HOURS/FEES: Sunrise–sunset; free. Café on the Beach is open 7:00 A.M.–5:00 P.M., except 7:00 A.M.–sunset Thursday through Sunday.

AMENITIES: Lifeguards, rest rooms, showers, volleyball, beach cafe, picnic tables, concrete pier.

ACTIVITIES: Surfing, volleyball, swimming, sunbathing, dining, picnicking, fishing.

FOR MORE INFORMATION: Manatee County Parks (941) 742–5923.

Egmont Key State Park

A tiny island smack in the mouth of Tampa Bay, the strategic location of Egmont Key has made it a witness to a great deal of history. The historic lighthouse was built in 1848, and was occupied by Confederate troops during the Civil War. When they found they stood no chance of defending their position against Union gunboats, the Confederates fled the island, taking the lighthouse's Fresnel lens with them. The missing lens was never recovered, though it was replaced with another. The Union troops used the island during their successful naval blockade of Tampa Bay.

Forty years later Egmont Key was put to military use again when the impending Spanish-American War led to the construction of Fort Dade, a minor paradise for those lucky enough to be stationed there. The 300 residents enjoyed electricity, telephones, a movie theater, bowling alley, tennis courts, and a hospital, though it lasted less than two decades before being decommissioned. You can walk through the ruins of the fort now, and along the brick paths.

The beach and surrounding waters are idyllic, available to those with a boat or by numerous ferry services. From January through May, guided walks are held on the second and fourth Sunday of each month, allowing visitors to tour the lighthouse and learn the entire history of the island.

ACCESS: By boat; the closest public launch ramp is Mullet Key on north side of Tampa Bay.

PARKING: Anchor off the beach.

HOURS/FEES: 8:00 A.M.–sunset; free.

AMENITIES: Lighthouse, historic fort walkways.

ACTIVITIES: Snorkeling, scuba diving, beach walking, lighthouse admiration, gopher tortoise viewing.

FOR MORE INFORMATION: Egmont Key State Park (727) 893–2627.

Cortez Lady (941) 761–9777 (departs from Cortez, south of Bradenton).

Captain Bill (727) 867–8168.

Captain Dave's (727) 367–4336.

Captain Frank's (727) 345–4500.

Captain Kidd (727) 360–2263.

Dolphin Landing (727) 360–7411.

Hubbards Sea Adventures (727) 398–6577 (departs from the St. Petersburg area and the beaches).

Shark's Teeth

Fossilized shark's teeth are one of the great finds of the Sarasota- and Venice-area beaches, and are plentiful. With luck you may even come up with the granddaddy of all shark's teeth, the huge beauties of the Megalodon shark. This long-extinct creature grew upward of 65 feet long, so you can imagine the size of the teeth. The nice thing about shark's teeth is they stand out in stark relief from the light-colored shells and grains around them: Wherever you search, just look for something black. The best time to look is after a recent storm, when the shifting sands have deposited a new layer.

Because these teeth are from so far back in history, modern notions of the Florida coast don't apply to where you may find them. One of the greatest areas for shark's teeth collecting is actually on the sandbars of the Peace River, 30 miles inland. With the drought Florida has suffered in recent years, the extremely low levels of the Peace have made it far easier for collectors to scour exposed bars for new finds.

A somewhat comical tale of another sort of treasure concerns the fictional pirate Jose Gaspar or Jose Gasparilla, after whom Gasparilla Island is named. Unfortunately, far too many people have taken the hoax seriously, and irrational treasure hunters have caused much destruction. A state park is even named after someone who never existed! An old fisherman named Johnny Gomez concocted the story in the late 1800s, selling maps and tips to the locations of the hidden gold of "Gasparilla." He claimed to have been a cabin boy on Gasparilla's ship and that a U.S. Navy ship had sunk Gasparilla's boat in the late 1820s. The story lived on far past Gomez's death, promulgated by real estate agents who saw a good way to sell area land. Even today, Tampa Bay merchants keep the story alive to sell their wares.

C rossing the Sunshine Skyway from the south, high up above Tampa Bay, you get a good look at the Gulf Coast's largest metropolitan area. Tampa occupies the interior end of the bay, which curves up to the north. The bay separates Tampa from the peninsula of St. Petersburg, which is where I–275 first deposits you before crossing the bay once again to reach Tampa. Home to a major international airport, pro baseball and football teams, the old Cuban settlement of Ybor City, and all kinds of museums and attractions, the Tampa Bay area has no lack of things to do.

Sunrise on Sand Key.

The beaches range from expansive county parks like Fort De Soto to charming old-time communities like Pass-a-Grille, along with modest beach accesses. In some places like Indian Shores Access, public beach has replaced one of the questionable glories of 1950s Florida, the wacky tropical theme park. Approaching Clearwater, Sand Key provides another vast expanse of county land to play on, surrounded by water on three sides.

The coastal road finally comes to an end north of Clearwater, though the barrier island stretches on past the development and is connected by a thin strip to the wonderful Caladesi Island State Park. There's no access from the southern end, though. You have to jog back inland and back out again to Honeymoon Island State Park, where you can catch a ferry over to Caladesi.

Access

From the south—Exit 4 off I–275 west to Pinellas Bayway.

From the north—West on SR 586/Curlew Avenue from US 19.

From the east—West on I–4 into Tampa; join I–275, take exit 21 north onto Veterans Expressway to exit 3, then go west on Hillsborough Memorial Highway to US 19.

Beaches

Fort De Soto County Park
Pass-a-Grille Beach
Treasure Island Beach
John's Pass Beach/Madeira Beach
Tiki Gardens–Indian Shores Access
Sand Key County Park
Caladesi Island State Park
Honeymoon Island State Park

Camping

Little Manatee River State Park—(813) 671–5005, off US 301 between Bradenton and Tampa. Camping is available at one of thirty-four sites, complete with electric and water hookups, set within a pristine sand pine scrub. Base rates are $10 from June through October, $12 from November through May. Electric hookups run $2.00 extra.

Fort De Soto County Park—(727) 582–2267. A 235-site family camping area with luxury facilities, including picnic tables, grills, water, electricity, washers, dryers, sanitary disposal stations, modern rest rooms, showers, play areas, and a camp store.

St. Petersburg/Madeira Beach Resort KOA—(727) 392–2233, in St. Petersburg just 2 miles from Madeira Beach. Tucked away on a mangrove-lined bayou with large sites in a tropical setting only 2 miles from Gulf beaches. Waterfront sites, sixty log Kamping Kabins, fishing dock, canoe, golf cart and bike rentals, pool, and three hot tubs. Rates are $30–37 for a two-person tent site.

Caladesi Island State Park—(727) 469–5918. Boat camping is available in the bayside marina for $8.00 per night.

Other Points of Interest

The Florida Aquarium—(813) 273–4000, 701 Channelside Drive, downtown Tampa. A glass dome standing three stories high offers exhibits on the diverse ecosystem and aquatic habitats of Florida. A variety of animals indigenous to the state are featured. Admission is $10.95 for the general public, and $5.95 for ages three through twelve. Parking is $3.00. Open 9:30 A.M.–5:00 P.M. daily from January 1 through Labor Day (until 9:00 P.M. on Friday from mid-June to mid-August) and mid-December through December 31; 10:00 A.M.–5:00 P.M. from the day after Labor Day to mid-December.

Lowry Park Zoological Garden—(813) 935–8552, 7530 North Boulevard, Tampa, right next to the Children's Museum of Tampa. Contains more than 350 animal species from four continents. Along with an extensive spread of land animals, the zoo has underground viewing rooms where visitors can catch a glimpse of some of the fascinating marine life that makes its home in Florida's waters. Open daily 9:30 A.M.–5:00 P.M.

The Museum of African-American Art—(813) 272–2466, just off I–275 at 1308 North Marion Street in Tampa. A variety of temporary and permanent exhibits with special events for the public year-round. Open 10:00 A.M.–4:30 P.M. Tuesday through Friday, 10:00 A.M.–5:00 P.M. Saturday.

The Museum of Science and Industry—(813) 987–6300, just before North 56th Street, 4801 East Fowler Avenue, Tampa. Provides visitors with more than 200,000 square feet of informative exhibits on science, industry, and technology. In addition, the Gulf Coast Hurricane gives patrons a chance to experience hurricane-force winds without running the danger of being squished by a flying mobile home. Open at 9:00 A.M. daily with varying closing times. Admission is $11.00 (includes tickets to the IMAX theater); $9.00 for visitors over fifty-nine, thirteen through eighteen, and college students with ID; $7.00 kids two through twelve.

The Ybor City Brewing Company—(813) 242–9222, 2205 North 20th Street, Ybor City, Tampa. Produces 15,000 barrels a year of Ybor Gold, Calusa Wheat, and Ybor Brown Ale. Housed in a former cigar factory, the recently established microbrewery offers a gift shop, tours, and product tasting. Open Tuesday through Saturday 11:00 A.M.–3:00 P.M. or by appointment. Admission is $2.00 per person.

The Salvador Dali Museum—(813) 823–3767, 1000 3rd Street South, St. Petersburg. Claims to be the largest collection of the Spanish artist's work. Admission $4.00 students with ID, $7.00 visitors over sixty-five, $8.00 general public, and free to children under ten.

Clearwater Marine Science Center Aquarium—(727) 441–1790, 249 Windward Passage, Clearwater. Dedicated to the care and rescue of sea turtles and sea mammals, the aquarium hosts exhibits on a variety of marine life. Open Monday through Friday 9:00 A.M.–5:00 P.M., Saturday 9:00 A.M.–4:00 P.M., Sunday 11:00 A.M.–4:00 P.M.

The Suncoast Seabird Sanctuary—(813) 391–6211, 18328 Gulf Boulevard, Indian Shores. Home to more than 500 sea- and land birds, and is also the site of America's largest wild-bird hospital. No charge for admissions, but donations are welcome. Open to the public daily 9:00 A.M.–sunset.

The Tampa Museum of Art—(813) 274–8130, 600 North Ashley Drive, Tampa. Exhibits permanent and traveling displays of Greek, Roman, and contemporary art. Open Tuesday through Saturday 10:00 A.M.–5:00 P.M. (Thursday until 8:00 P.M.) and Sunday 1:00–5:00 P.M. Admissions for adults $5.00; senior citizens $4.00; students with ID and kids over six $3.00, kids under six free.

The Ybor City State Museum—(813) 987–6771, 1818 9th Avenue, Ybor City, Tampa. Covers the cigar industry in Cuba of the mid–nineteenth century as well as Ybor City's history as a world-class cigar manufacturing center. Open Tuesday through Saturday 9:00 A.M.–noon and 1:00–5:00 P.M. Admission is $2.00. There is no charge for children under six.

Tiki Gardens–Indian Shores Access.

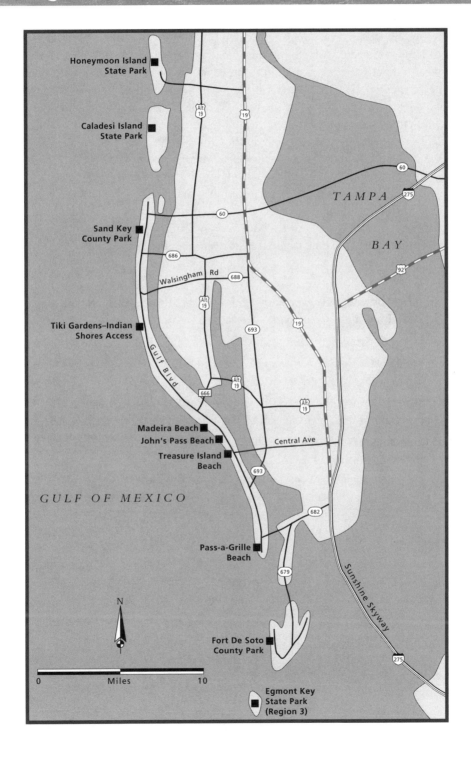

Honeymoon Island
State Park

Caladesi Island
State Park

Alt 19

19

TAMPA

60

275

BAY

60

Sand Key
County Park

686

Walsingham Rd

688

92

Alt 19

693

19

Tiki Gardens–Indian
Shores Access

Gulf Blvd

Alt 19

666

Alt 19

Madeira Beach
John's Pass Beach
Central Ave
Treasure Island
Beach

693

GULF OF MEXICO

682

Pass-a-Grille
Beach

679

Sunshine Skyway

N

Fort De Soto
County Park

275

0   Miles   10

Egmont Key
State Park
(Region 3)

Fort De Soto County Park

About everything you could want to go to the beach for is available on the five interconnected islands of this Pinellas County park. It's one of the favorite family excursion areas for Tampa locals. At the fort after which the park is named, there is a battery of 12-inch mortars, and some more recently added British breechloading cannons from 1890. For fishermen there are boat ramps with docks, and two fishing piers—the one fronting on Tampa Bay is 500 feet long and the one on the Gulf is 1,000 feet.

Though the Gulf waters are inviting enough, those looking for lifeguards and a more controlled environment can use the two swimming pool centers at North Beach. The beaches are beautiful white sand, extending for 3 miles around the north and east ends. There are many ways to get around, from strolling with the sand between your toes to skating or biking on the 4-mile recreation trail. A 2-mile canoe trail also weaves among the islands.

ACCESS: Exit I–275 west onto SR 682/Pinellas Bayway on the north side of Sunshine Skyway. Drive 2.5 miles to SR 679, turn left, and go south 6 miles to the park.

PARKING: Multiple parking lots.

HOURS/FEES: Sunrise–sunset; 85-cent road toll.

AMENITIES: Rest rooms, showers, campground, picnic shelters, grills, boat ramp, floating docks, fishing piers, paved bike paths, canoe trail, hiking trail, historic cannons.

ACTIVITIES: Fishing, camping, biking, skating, picnicking, beach walking, sunbathing, canoeing.

FOR MORE INFORMATION: Fort De Soto Park (727) 866–2484.

Pass-a-Grille Beach

Located on the southernmost barrier island of the St. Pete beaches, this is one of the quieter areas along this bustling stretch. The island opened up when Roy S. Hanna and Tampa cigar magnate Selwyn Morey began developing it in the 1880s, and it became home to fishermen, homesteaders, and lumber men. The town of Pass-a-Grille is a nice old seaside Florida town, one of those places that time forgot in the surrounding development, partly because the village is but one block wide and thirty-one blocks long. There are lifeguards on the beach, and plenty of room. You can take a sunset cruise or ride a ferry out to Shell Key for beachcombing.

A new trolley system that started operating in 2001 has made access to Pass-a-Grille and the other area beaches much easier, and eliminated many of the traffic headaches you used to face in navigating the congestion of the Tampa/St. Pete area. Running from Pass-a-Grille up to Sand Key, with connections inland to St. Petersburg, the trolleys run every half hour from 5:45 A.M. to 10:10 P.M. Monday through Sunday. The fare is a dollar per trip, and seven-day unlimited passes cost only $12.

ACCESS: Exit I–275 west onto SR 682/Pinellas Bayway on the north side of Sunshine Skyway. Drive 4 miles to SR 699/Gulf Boulevard, turn left, and continue south for a mile.

PARKING: Metered parking for twenty blocks, from 1st to 21st Avenues.

HOURS/FEES: Sunrise–sunset, 50-cent road toll, $1.00-per-hour parking.

AMENITIES: Lifeguards, rest rooms, showers, food concessions.

ACTIVITIES: Sun worshiping, swimming.

FOR MORE INFORMATION: St. Pete Beach Parks (727) 367–2735.
Shell Key Shuttle (727) 360–1348; www.shellkeyshuttle.com.

Treasure Island Beach

This is a small one-acre beach park near the Treasure Island Causeway. It's a great beach—if you can get parking. Because it's one of the first beach outlets from downtown St. Petersburg, it fills up very fast. The smartest thing to do is take the PSTA trolley from one of the other beaches, or take a bus from St. Petersburg. There are plenty of restaurants and shops close by, so you can shower, get changed, and walk across the street to eat.

ACCESS: From US 19 in downtown St. Petersburg, head west on Central Avenue to the Treasure Island Causeway and drive across to Gulf Boulevard. Turn left and go three blocks to 104th Avenue.

PARKING: Sixty-seven spaces.

HOURS/FEES: 5:00 A.M.–1:00 A.M.; free.

AMENITIES: Rest rooms, showers, bicycle rack.

ACTIVITIES: Sunbathing, swimming.

FOR MORE INFORMATION: Treasure Island Beach (727) 549–6165.

John's Pass Beach/Madeira Beach

As you come off the Tom Stuart Causeway from St. Petersburg, Madeira Beach is the first public access you encounter. A pleasant county park lined with cabbage palms and sea oats, it only takes up 450 feet of beachfront, though there's nothing stopping you from enjoying the beach to the south or north. In fact, if you walk along the beach for fifteen blocks to the south, you come to another public beach, John's Pass Beach. The town of John's Pass is a bustling tourist village, full of seafood restaurants and maritime charm. There's a 1,000-foot boardwalk to walk along, and various tour boats, cruises, and fishing charters run out of the marina. Bicycles are a good way to enjoy this stretch, or you can use the PSTA trolley that runs between Sand Key and Pass-a-Grille.

Madeira Beach.

ACCESS: From US 19 or I–275, head west on 5th Avenue in downtown St. Petersburg to Alternate 19/595. Drive 5 miles to CR 666, cross the Tom Stuart Causeway, turn left onto Gulf Boulevard and go south to 144th Avenue for Madeira Beach, or 129th Avenue for John's Pass.

PARKING: You'll find 104 metered spaces at Madeira Beach and a metered lot at John's Beach.

HOURS/FEES: 5:00 A.M.–midnight at John's Pass, 7:00 A.M.–sunset at Madeira; $1.00 per hour.

AMENITIES: Rest rooms, showers, picnic tables, bicycle rack.

ACTIVITIES: Sunbathing, swimming, fishing.

FOR MORE INFORMATION: John's Pass (727) 391–1611.

Madeira Beach Access (727) 549–6165.

✳ ✳ ⚊

Tiki Gardens–Indian Shores Access

A fairly recent county acquisition, Indian Shores Access is midway between St. Petersburg and Clearwater. As such, it draws a little less of a crowd and has a good amount of parking. The public beach has replaced the old Tiki Gardens theme park, a re-creation of a South Seas paradise that "Trader Frank" Byars and his wife Jo built in 1963. It was a bizarre park, sprawling with giant tikis, monkeys, and birds. Equally unique was its design, presented to builders on brown wrapping paper as they thought new things up. Trader Frank sold it in 1988, and the county opened it as a public park in 1995. With a spacious beach and a nice trail through beautiful landscaping, it's rapidly becoming a new favorite.

ACCESS: From US 19 between Pinellas Park and Clearwater, head west on SR 688/Ulmerton Road for 8 miles to Indian Rocks Beach. Turn left onto SR 699/Gulf Boulevard and continue 2.5 miles south to a parking area on your left.

PARKING: There are 170 metered spaces in two lots on the east side of Gulf Boulevard.

HOURS/FEES: 7:00 A.M.–sunset; 50 cents per hour.

AMENITIES: Rest rooms, showers, benches.

ACTIVITIES: Sunbathing, swimming.

FOR MORE INFORMATION: Indian Shores Access (727) 549–6165.

Tiki Gardens (727) 595–2567.

Suncoast Seabird Sanctuary (727) 391–6211.

Tiki Gardens.

Heading south away from the crowded public beaches of Clearwater is one of the largest parks in Pinellas County. Located on the south side of Clearwater Pass Bridge, Sand Key is a top-notch facility. There's more than 2,000 feet of beachfront, lifeguards, and a lot of room to roam. It's a great picnicking area, and families take advantage of its spaciousness. Interestingly enough, the shifting sands around the pass keep adding to the beach. More than twenty-five acres have been added to the park in the past decade due to natural build-up. Though the park gets well over a million visitors a year, the parking areas are so extensive that the place rarely seems crowded.

ACCESS: From US 19 in Clearwater, drive west on SR 60/Gulf-to-Bay Boulevard for 7 miles to Clearwater Beach. Turn left onto SR 699/Gulf Boulevard and continue 1.5 miles south to a parking area on your right.

PARKING: 794 metered spaces in lots.

HOURS/FEES: 7:00 A.M.–sunset; 75 cents per hour.

AMENITIES: Lifeguards, rest rooms, showers, picnic tables, food concessions.

ACTIVITIES: Sunbathing, swimming, surfing, beach walking.

FOR MORE INFORMATION: Sand Key County Park (727) 588–4852.

Sunbathing at Sand Key.

Caladesi Island State Park

Caladesi Island is one of those gorgeous barrier island state parks like Cayo Costa on the lower Gulf, untouched by development and maintained as a boat-only access park. Though the park is comprised of six islands, Caladesi Island is the main part. The island separated itself from Honeymoon Island to the north after a monster hurricane in 1921 ripped open the channel now known as Hurricane Pass. Actually, Caladesi isn't even quite an island of its own, since it's still connected by a thin strip on the south end to Clearwater Beach Island. There is no access from this end, however.

The beaches are wonderfully pristine, graced with rolling sand dunes covered in sea oats. The park is a nature lover's delight, since the interior contains an old maritime hammock of soaring sabal palms, southern red cedar, and live oak. From its limbs, the latter drips the ubiquitous Spanish moss that so symbolizes old Florida. Nature trails lead from the marina on the bay side of the island through this hammock to the beaches. Gopher tortoises make their homes in sand burrows, and you have to keep an eye and ear out in the woods for the eastern diamondback rattlesnake. A chance meeting with one is extremely unlikely, however.

The ninety-nine slip marina is the main hub of facilities, though you'll find rest rooms and picnic shelters elsewhere in the park. While there is no camping on the island, boat camping is allowed at the marina. In addition, a regular ferry from Honeymoon Island brings visitors over.

ACCESS: From US 19 in Dunedin, head west on SR 586/Curlew Road for 5 miles to Honeymoon Island State Park. Then take the ferry.

PARKING: Ninety-nine boat slips in a bayside marina on Caladesi, car parking for the ferry at Honeymoon Island.

HOURS/FEES: 8:00 A.M.–sunset; $1.00 per hiker or biker, $2.00 per single-occupant vehicle, $4.00 per vehicle with two to eight passengers. The ferry runs $6.00 per adult round trip, $3.50 for those four through twelve; under three are free. It's $3.25 for a private boat, $8.00 overnight boat camping.

AMENITIES: Rest rooms, showers, picnic areas, boardwalks, nature trails, playground, beach chair and umbrella rentals.

ACTIVITIES: Sunbathing, swimming, boating, fishing, shelling, boat camping, hiking, bird-watching.

FOR MORE INFORMATION: Caladesi Island State Park (727) 469–5918.

Ferry information (727) 734–5263.

Ferry schedules (727) 734–1501.

Honeymoon Island State Park

Honeymoon Island has a rich and diverse history, from its settlement by Tocobagan Indians, to its use by Spanish colonizers, to the mix of pirates, traders, and nomadic fishermen that populated it in the early 1800s. The island changed names from Sand Island to Hog Island in the latter part of the nineteenth century after a successful hog farm was established. In 1921 it was separated from Caladesi Island by a hurricane, and soon began being pitched by developers as Honeymoon Island. Before World War II, newsreels and magazine ads showed off thatched bungalows in a subtropical paradise, and urged newlyweds to come. The development dream never quite got off the ground, though, since it was requisitioned as an R&R base for soldiers after America entered the war. Thankfully, the variety of schemes planned for it by a succession of developers never quite jelled, and there are still rare stands of virgin slash pine in the forests of the island.

The beach goes on and on, beginning on the south side of the island, then wrapping around to the west and up north to Pelican Point. For adventurous kayakers, there are a few other small islands off the northern end that you can paddle to. The park also features one of the only "pet beaches" in the state, where dog owners can legally let their pets play. There's excellent fishing around the island, along with hiking trails and plenty of birding opportunities.

ACCESS: From US 19 in Dunedin, head west on SR 586/Curlew Road
5 miles to Honeymoon Island.

PARKING: Free parking lots.

HOURS/FEES: 8:00 A.M.–sunset; $1.00 per hiker or biker, $2.00 per single-occupant vehicle, $4.00 per vehicle with two to eight passengers.

AMENITIES: Rest rooms, showers, picnic areas, food concession, volleyball courts, nature trails, pet beach.

ACTIVITIES: Sunbathing, swimming, fishing, volleyball, pet play, beach walking, hiking, bird-watching.

FOR MORE INFORMATION: Honeymoon Island State Recreation Area (727) 469–5942.

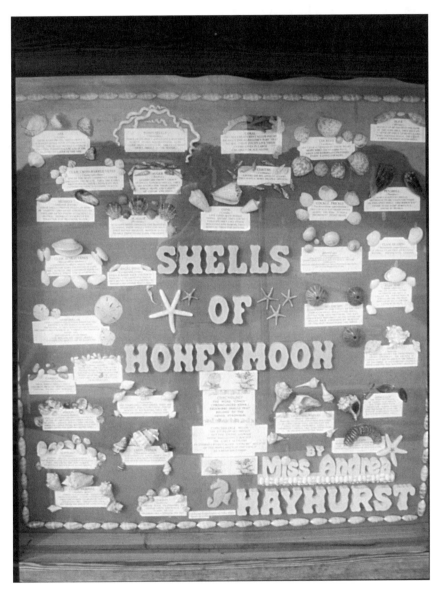

Honeymoon Island.

Sand Fleas

These small crustaceans are a curious part of the shoreline habitat. Not to be confused with sand flies, the biting no-see-um insects that are the bane of many a Floridian's existence, the sand flea is the bait of choice of surf fishermen throughout Florida. Grouping together in large colonies, sand fleas burrow into the sand at the water's edge. It's a strange sight when you come across them in droves, wiggling through the sand as a wave washes out. Fishermen collect them with a rake fitted with a wire mesh basket at the bottom. You walk along the water's edge, raking up basketfuls of sand and then shaking it loose through the bottom of the mesh. If you're lucky, you'll get dozens of the little hard-shell amphipods. They're pretty much the best bait you can use for catching pompano, which is considered one of the finest-tasting fish in the state. My middle-school basketball coach, Coach McClane, called them "seafleas." With a rich laugh for the silly modern rod-and-reel methods of his white students, he claimed the only true way to fish them was with a long cane pole.

Some of my earliest memories are of a beach somewhere on the Gulf Coast, digging in the sand for these creatures. I consulted my parents to help me flesh out this elusive vision, and they told me they had handed me off to my aunt Janet and some family friends for a visit to a favorite old beach hotel north of Naples. The place was Vanderbilt Beach, which was a virtually empty stretch of coastline at the time and now adjoins Delnor-Wiggins State Park.

Depending on the time of year, sand flea collecting can be a lucrative business. (Haven't you always dreamed of telling people that you're a "sand flea collector"?) When they're hard to come by, bait and tackle shops will pay extraordinary amounts of money for a bucketful of them. In turn, they'll sell them by the dozen and quintuple their outlay. While it may have an immediate appeal, after an eight-hour day of hard work to collect a single bucket, you may well be thinking of hanging on to your day job.

Region 5

W hile the Big Bend of Florida is certainly big, beaches are not its strong suit. The coastline becomes shallow tidal estuary, and sand all but disappears except for a few protruding peninsulas and off-shore islands. Howard Park is somewhere between the two, connected by a causeway to the mainland just south of the mouth of the Anclote River. Offshore, the Anclote Keys are a boat-only paradise. These are still part of Pinellas County, though, and not really part of the Big Bend.

When you leave the unfortunate civilization of Pasco County behind and travel US 19 out of Hudson and on up toward Weeki Wachee, you're entering

Howard Park.

the Big Bend. This is the land of the infinite wilderness. Gorgeous springs, wild rivers, shallow bays, towns that barely register until you're through them—and often not even then—this neck of the woods is a nature lover's delight. The population density is so low it's ridiculous. Fort Island Beach in Crystal River is the last place the highway goes close to the coast, before it veers well inland.

One of the lovelier set of islands in the state is the Cedar Keys National Wildlife Refuge, just offshore of the town of Cedar Key. After its nineteenth-century boom times, this town wallowed in peaceful obscurity for the following hundred years. A long empty road runs all the way out from Gainesville to Cedar Key, which everyone used to call the Swamp Road. It seemed like a mysterious dead end. Access to the coast is like this throughout the Big Bend: tiny county roads off the main highway that lead to equally tiny outposts on the Gulf. Scalloping is a big pastime in the shallow waters, which you can wade in for ages without getting deeper than your waist.

Many visitors make the mistake of ignoring places like the Big Bend because there doesn't appear to be anything there. Away from the beaches, Florida is a difficult mystery to penetrate unless you know where to go. All the truly magical places like the springs and rivers are hidden from view. The flatness of the state and the canopies of forest do a marvelous job of hiding countless secrets from most of the world.

Access

From the south—Take exit 30 off I–275 and go west on SR 580 to US 19. Turn right and go north to Tarpon Springs.

From the north—Take exit 35 off I–10 south to Perry on US 221, and join US 98.

Beaches

Howard Park
Anclote Keys Preserve State Park
Fort Island Beach
Cedar Keys National Wildlife Refuge
Keaton Beach aka Hodges Park

Camping

Anclote Keys Preserve State Park—(727) 469–5918. Primitive camping with more than seventy-five campsites on a pine ridge in the center of the park. Modern facilities and a dump station are on the premises.

Citrus County Chassahowitzka River Campground—(352) 382–2200, on the Chassahowitzka River. A 40-acre campground within walking distance of a 30,000-acre national wildlife refuge. Enjoy the spring-fed Chassahowitzka River by boat, canoe, or biking trails. Has eighty-eight sites; full hookups for self-contained vehicles are available as well as separate and secluded tent sites. Bathhouse, Laundromat, cold soft drinks. Boat and canoe rentals are also offered. Pets welcomed. Rates are $14 for rustic, $16 for water/electric, $18 for full hookups.

Sunset Isles RV Park—(352) 543–5375, (800) 810–1103. Located 1.3 miles from downtown Cedar Key. Walk or bike to the heart of downtown. Five fishing docks, lots of birds to watch. Tent sites for two people run $20 per night for one night, $12 per night for two or more.

Waccasassa Bay State Preserve—(352) 543–5567, east of Cedar Key. Primitive campsites along Waccasassa River. First come, first served.

Manatee Springs State Park—(352) 493–6072, off US 98 on the Suwannee River, 35 miles west of Gainesville. Manatee Spring is a first-magnitude spring pumping 117 million gallons of crystal-clear water into the Suwannee River daily. The park has a hundred-site campground with electricity and water in each site. These sites are available for tenters or RVers. There are comfort stations centrally located in each of the loops. Comfort stations provide hot showers, toilets, and sink facilities. Rates are $11.00 per night, $2.00 more for electric.

Keaton Beach Campground—(800) 589–1541, at Keaton Beach. From tent camping to full hookups. The store is fully stocked with fresh- and saltwater fishing supplies, fresh and frozen bait, hardware, and camping gear. It is also home to the Gas & Grill deli, so you can fish instead of cook. Less than a mile from the beach and 2 miles from excellent bass fishing at Blue Springs Lake. Bathrooms and showers; pets on leashes are welcome. Rates are $10 with water, $12 with electric, $16 with water and electric; $18 for full hookups.

Other Points of Interest

Homosassa Springs State Wildlife Park—(352) 628–2311, 75 miles north of Tampa off US 19. View manatees in crystal-clear water from an underwater observatory. Visit a Florida black bear, bobcats, alligators, foxes, and otters. Gift shops, boat transportation, restaurant, and visitor center. Some of the most beautiful springs in Florida.

Crystal River State Archaeological Site—(352) 795–3817, on Museum Point in Crystal River. A six-mound complex built by pre-Columbian Mound

Builders. For 1,600 years this site was occupied, with Native Americans traveling great distances to bury their dead here and hold ceremonies.

Yulee Sugar Mill Ruins State Historic Site—(352) 795–3817, in Homosasssa 75 miles north of Tampa. A 5,100-acre sugar plantation owned by David Yulee, a U.S. senator in the mid-1800s and one of the great developers of early Florida.

Chassahowitzka Springs/National Wildlife Refuge—(352) 563–2088. Located about 65 miles north of St. Petersburg, the Chassahowitzka National Wildlife Refuge is comprised of more than 31,000 acres of saltwater bays, estuaries, and brackish marshes with a fringe of hardwood swamps along the eastern boundary. The northern boundary parallels and includes much of the Homosassa River. The refuge extends southward across the scenic Chassahowitzka River for 12 miles to its southern boundary at Raccoon Point.

Waccasassa Bay State Preserve—(352) 543–5567, east of Cedar Key. This 30,000-acre preserve is a gigantic area of salt marsh, woods, and tidal creeks. Very wild and quiet; great for canoeing and adventuring. A small remnant of the vast Gulf Hammock, one of the largest natural areas of old Florida.

Econfina River State Park—(850) 922–6007, on SR 19 south of US 98, about 50 miles southeast of Tallahassee. Woods and salt marsh, similar to the other coastal areas of the Big Bend.

San Marcos de Apalache State Historic Site—(850) 922–6007, off SR 363 in St. Marks, 30 miles south of Tallahassee. Site of a 1679 fort at the confluence of the Wakulla and St. Marks Rivers. A museum explains the history of the settlement, first reached in 1528 by Panfilo de Narvaez and his 300 men.

On-shore fishing.

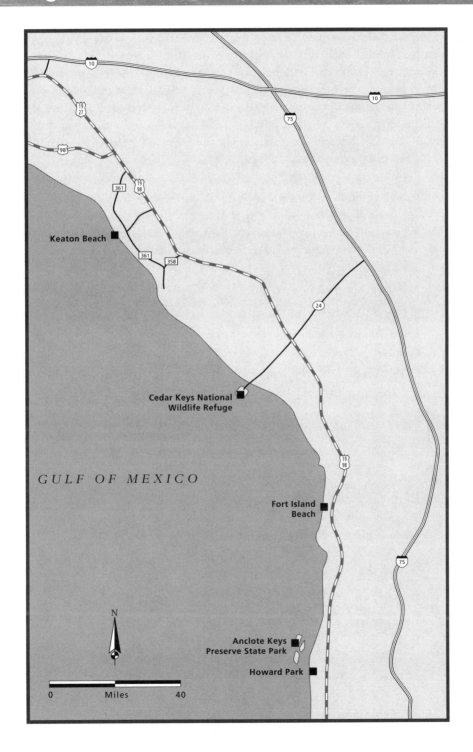

Keaton Beach

Cedar Keys National
Wildlife Refuge

GULF OF MEXICO

Fort Island
Beach

N

Anclote Keys
Preserve State Park

Howard Park

0   Miles   40

Howard Park

Howard Park draws people from many miles around because it's the only quality public beach accessible by mainland in northern Pinellas County. Furthermore, most of the population of Pasco County comes down here to swim because of their lack of decent beaches. The 155-acre park is connected to the mainland by a mile-long causeway, and sailboarders love the shallow bay in between. The beach is 1,000 feet long and scenic, with views of the Anclote Keys in the distance. On the mainland side there's a softball field and playground, along with picnic areas with plenty of shade.

ACCESS: From US 19, turn west onto Tarpon Avenue in Tarpon Springs and go 1 mile west, across Alternate 19 to where Tarpon Avenue ends at Spring Boulevard. Turn right onto Spring Boulevard and follow the winding road until you reach Sunset Drive (CR 944). Take Sunset Drive west to the park.

PARKING: Free parking lots.

HOURS/FEES: Sunrise–sunset, free.

AMENITIES: Rest rooms, showers, picnic tables, softball field, playground.

ACTIVITIES: Sailboarding, sunbathing, swimming, picnicking.

FOR MORE INFORMATION: Howard Park (727) 943–4031.

Howard Park.

Anclote Keys Preserve State Park

Geologically, the Anclote Keys are one of the youngest areas in Florida. The keys were only pushed off the Gulf seafloor 1,000 years ago, and have even increased in size by a third in the past fifty years. Located 3 miles offshore of Tarpon Springs, they are a popular destination for area boaters, and boat is the only way to access them.

Though powerboat is the fastest way of reaching the park, an enthusiastic kayaker can launch from Howard Park and paddle a little over 2 miles of open water to the southern tip and the Anclote Keys Lighthouse. A GPS would be advisable to make navigation more sure, though the steady rush of powerboats back and forth from Tarpon Springs is usually a pretty good reference. The natural state of the islands is delicate, and visitors are encouraged to leave a minimum of disturbance behind. Forty-three species of birds are found here, from plovers to bald eagles, making it a favorite of birders.

Anclote Keys.

Like many of the offshore barrier islands, there is a higher ridge in the center of the island; camping is allowed on this ridge of pine forest and maritime hammock.

ACCESS: Launch a powerboat from Sunset Beach west of Tarpon Springs or at Robert Rees Park west of New Port Richey; canoe or kayak 2 miles from Howard Park west of Tarpon Springs.

PARKING: Anchor off the beach.

HOURS/FEES: 8:00 A.M.–sunset; free.

AMENITIES: None.

ACTIVITIES: Sunbathing, swimming, boating, fishing, shelling, primitive camping, hiking, bird-watching.

FOR MORE INFORMATION: Anclote Keys Preserve State Park (727) 469–5918.

Island Wind Tours (727) 934–0606.

Sunset Beach (727) 942–5610.

Howard Park (727) 943–4031.

Anclote Keys.

Fort Island Beach

As you move up the Gulf Coast toward the Big Bend area, beaches become a rare commodity. Fort Island is the best mainland beach to be found until you get all the way up into the Panhandle. There's 1,000 feet of beachfront, summer lifeguards, a volleyball court, and nice picnic shelters and barbecue facilities. Located near the town of Crystal River, it's a bonus having a nice beach to visit in an area stocked with a lot of other attractions. Crystal River is one of the most popular places in Florida for swimming with endangered manatees; you can snorkel in the crystal-clear waters of the springs that the manatees inhabit during winter months. Out in the waters of Kings Bay, leading into the Gulf, Crystal River National Wildlife Refuge provides a home to 20 percent of the Florida manatee population. It is among these islands and shallows that the manatees spend the warmer months of the year. Fort Island Beach has a boat ramp that accesses the bay waters, as well as providing direct access to the Gulf of Mexico.

ACCESS: From US 19 just south of Crystal River, head west on SR 44/Fort Island Trail for 9 miles.

HOURS/FEES: Sunrise–sunset; free.

AMENITIES: Boat ramp, volleyball court, rest rooms, showers, picnic shelters, grills, summer lifeguards.

ACTIVITIES: Boating, sunbathing, swimming, picnicking.

FOR MORE INFORMATION: Citrus County Parks (352) 795–2202.

Crystal River Chamber of Commerce (352) 795–3149.

Crystal River State Archaeological Site (352) 795–3817.

Snorkeling at Fort Island Beach.

The town of Cedar Key had a fascinating role in the development of Florida, though looking at the tiny town of 800 residents, you'd never guess. David Levy Yulee, a two-term U.S. senator who had large sugar and slave interests, was responsible for the railroad that linked Cedar Key to Fernandina on the east coast in 1861. The railroad was a chance to export sugar, timber, and cotton, and made Cedar Key a boomtown along the lines of Key West. Hundreds of thousands of people were visiting Cedar Key by the late 1880s, and it did live up to Yulee's dreams briefly. Unfortunately, the rush for riches neglected some basic facts about replenishable resources. Eagle Pencils cut down all the cedar forests and then left town. The boom came crashing to a halt, and the town fell back into obscurity. In 1896 the town was wiped off the face of the earth by a killer hurricane, with the 1861-built Island Hotel being one of the only structures to survive through to today.

Tourism has steadily increased in the area over the past few decades, thanks in large part to the rich, natural attractions of the Cedar Keys

Cedar Key.

National Wildlife Refuge. The refuge is comprised of twelve outlying barrier islands near the town. Seahorse Key, which sits farthest out in the Gulf, has been used as a military hospital and served as a detention camp during the Seminole Wars. A lighthouse lasted for a century on the island before being abandoned, and is now a marine research center for the University of Florida. What makes the island truly unique is that it's a giant sand dune that rises all the way to 52 feet in the center, the highest point on the Gulf Coast of Florida. The other islands also have central ridges that are home to dense maritime hammocks of live oak, red bay, and sabal palms. The interiors of all the islands are closed to the public, however.

The beaches are open on all the keys year-round to visitors, with the exception of Seahorse Key, and they are some of the most gorgeous wilderness beaches in Florida. Seahorse Key is closed from March through June to protect nesting birds. The largest colonial rookery in north Florida is located on Seahorse Keys, and the bird life on all the keys is abundant. Kayaks are a great way to get around the islands; otherwise you can find your boat high and dry when the tides recede.

ACCESS: From US 19/98, drive west on SR 24 for 15 miles to Cedar Key. Take boat shuttles from the Cedar Key Docks; the public boat ramp is on the tip of the mainland before you cross the causeway to Cedar Key.

PARKING: Free parking for boat shuttles.

HOURS/FEES: Sunrise–sunset; free.

AMENITIES: Lighthouse/Marine Science Laboratory on Seahorse Key, rest room on Atsena Otie Key.

ACTIVITIES: Boating, sunbathing, swimming, shell collecting, bird watching.

FOR MORE INFORMATION: Cedar Keys National Wildlife Refuge (352) 493–0238.

Island Hopper Boat Tours (352) 543–5904.

Wild Florida Adventures (kayak rental).

Toll free (877) 945–3928.

Local (352) 373–6047 tours@wild-florida.com.

Cedar Key State Museum, open Thursday–Monday, 9:00 A.M.–5:00 P.M., (352) 543–5350.

Keaton Beach aka Hodges Park

Though not a typical sort of Gulf beach destination, Keaton Beach has a certain charm unique to the Big Bend of Florida. The Big Bend is one of the greatest places to go scalloping in Florida, and a day at Keaton Beach is a fine place to pursue this activity. If you love these tasty shellfish but don't like spending $10 a pound on them, you might enjoy gathering them yourself. There's a free boat ramp across the street from the campground, which is billed as the only free deep-water access ramp in Taylor County. There's another at Blue Springs along Blue Creek, which is a great place to swim and rinse off at the end of a salty day on the Gulf. Blue Springs Lake has good bass fishing.

Keaton Beach was devastated by the 1993 winter storm that shut down much of the East Coast, when a tidal surge roared through the community and flattened virtually everything in its path. It's one of the most remote and quiet areas you can find in Florida, surrounded to the north and south by more than 1,000 square miles with virtually no people. When Gainesville locals want to spend a Saturday escaping the madness that accompanies University of Florida football, this is one of the places they come.

ACCESS: From US 19/98/27A, drive 2 miles south of Perry, then head south on CR 361 for 12 miles to Keaton Beach.

PARKING: Parking lot.

HOURS/FEES: Sunrise–sunset; free.

AMENITIES: Rest rooms, picnic shelters.

ACTIVITIES: Sunbathing, swimming, scalloping, fishing.

FOR MORE INFORMATION: Taylor County Parks (352) 838–3528.

Enjoying beach solitude.

Homosassa or Chassahowitzka?

Confronted with this choice of destinations, most people unfamiliar with the Gulf Coast of Florida would simply say: Huh? Located within 10 miles of each other, approximately 75 miles north of Tampa, these two sets of springs are home to a lot more than clear water. Homosassa Springs State Wildlife Park is the only place in Florida where you can watch manatees in their natural environment from behind glass walls, as well as see bobcats, panthers, Florida black bears, and other indigenous wildlife. The name *Homosassa* means "place where wild pepper grows" in the Creek language, and the centerpiece of the park is the 45-foot-deep natural spring that serves as the headwaters of the Homosassa River.

The plantation owner and state senator David Levy Yulee, who played such a major role in the development of Cedar Key, owned a sugar plantation and refinery along the Homosassa River in the 1850s. He employed 1,000 people, but his mansion was burned by Union troops during the Civil War and the sugar mill shut down. Today the mill is a state historic site. The Homosassa-to-Ocala train line became known as the "Mullet Express," because it carried barrels filled with mullet and ice inland. During Prohibition, those barrels carried moonshine as well. In 1941 the track and depot were retired, and the commercial life of Homosassa came to an end.

Chassahowitzka means "the pumpkin opening place" or "place of the hanging pumpkins" in the Seminole language. The springs flow into the Chassahowitzka River, which flows out into the Gulf through the 30,000-acre expanse of the Chassahowitzka National Wildlife Refuge. It's a wild and remote area with no roads, and the whole area up through Crystal River becomes an important sanctuary for the West Indian manatee. These lovable underwater cousins of the elephant are rarely seen in clear water except for the springs they retreat to in winter when the Gulf gets too cold. Homosassa, Chassahowitzka, and Crystal River are prime viewing areas during winter and offer a good look at them. They're very loving and gentle, and watching them frolic with each other and their young is always a delight. Because they must eat 10 to 15 percent of their body weight every day to survive, they spend most of their time in shallow bays chewing on musk grass. Due to their inability to avoid motorboats, it is essential that you travel at idle speeds when in manatee areas. Propeller wounds are the greatest cause of manatee deaths each year, and the number of manatees has diminished to a critical level in Florida.

E merging from the Big Bend into the Forgotten Coast of the Panhandle, you enter the "island zone." Most of the beaches here are on offshore islands or peninsulas, and they're some of the most breathtaking strips of sand in Florida. Unlike the sands of the lower Gulf, which are usually off white to darker colors, the Panhandle beaches are dazzling white powder sand. Definitely keep your sunglasses on. Almost all the parks are state or federal lands, and as such are managed to keep the dunes and the natural splendor as pristine as possible.

The mainland towns are steps back in time, old fishing communities like Apalachicola and Carrabelle that have weathered many hurricanes and still endure. The seafood festival at Apalachicola in the first week of November is an incredible culinary experience. Late fall is quite a nice time to visit in general. The air has started getting brisk, which makes long beach walks more enjoyable, and the water is still tolerable for swimming. In addition, cabins at some of the state parks are a bargain then.

The "beaches of the Saints"—George, Vincent, and Joseph—are remarkable wilderness areas that offer endless pleasures to those who love exploring. Whether it be by kayak, powerboat, bicycle, or foot, there are always new nooks and crannies. Almost half the beaches in this region are accessible only by boat. For people looking for nightlife, a social scene, or anything involving other people, you might want to go farther west in the Panhandle. For folks looking to forget about the world, the Forgotten Coast is the place.

Access

From the north/east—Take exit 29 or 30 off I–10 south through Tallahassee to US 319, then south to US 98, and west into Carrabelle.

From the north/west—From exit 21 off I–10, go south on SR 71 for 40 miles to US 98 in Port St. Joe. Continue south on SR 30 to Cape San Blas.

Beaches

Dog Island
St. George Island State Park
Cape St. George State Reserve aka Little St. George
St. Vincent National Wildlife Refuge
Salinas Park
Cape Palms Park
St. Joseph Peninsula State Park

Camping

St. George Island State Park—(850) 927–2111. Sixty campsites in a campground located in the pine forests on the bay side. There are primitive campsites at Gap Point for those who wish to hike the 2.5-mile trail. Base rate $8.00 per night from September through January, $14.00 from February through August; $2.00 extra for electric.

Cape St. George Preserve—(850) 927–2111. Primitive camping is permitted at designated sites at West Pass, Sikes Cut, and the Government Dock. Boat access only.

Hickory Landing/Owl Creek—Fifteen miles north of Apalachicola on SR 65, turn left (west) onto Forest Service Road 101 for 1.5 miles, then turn left onto Forest Service Road 101-B for 1 mile. Picturesque camping and fishing among beautiful cypress stands. Camping (ten units), picnicking, sanitary facilities, drinking water, excellent fishing and canoeing along Owl Creek, boat-launching facilities, access to the Apalachicola River. Free!

Cape San Blas Camping Resort—(850) 229–6800, capesanblas@aol.com. Located 1.5 miles out on the cape, 10 miles south of Port St. Joe, along a stretch of white-sand beach facing due south. Thirty-six campsites are situated among natural Florida beach scrub with a combination of palm, pine, and scrub oak trees. There's a computer laptop station with phone connection at the office for e-mail access (local or 800 calls only). Fax machine, two pay telephones, pool, groceries, laundry, canoe rentals, fishing rentals. Rates March through October are $12–14 rustic, $14–16 with full hookups; 20 percent off November through February.

St. Joseph Peninsula State Park—(850) 227–1327. This campground has 119 sites with full hookups, $15.00–17.00 from March through October, $8.00–10.00 from November through February. Primitive camping in the wilderness preserve section is $3.00 for adults, $2.00 for those seven to eighteen years old; free under six. Cabins are $70 per night from March to mid-September, $55 per night from mid-September through February.

Other Points of Interest

Ochlockonee River State Park—(850) 962–2771. Fifteen miles northeast of Carrabelle, 10 miles north of the coast. Fishing, canoe rental, and boat ramp, along with two riverside campgrounds.

John Gorrie Museum—(850) 653–9347, in Apalachicola. Historical exhibits about the area. Replica of the first ice-making machine.

Apalachicola Seafood Festival—First weekend of November. Great time to visit this area and sample the incredible bounty of seafood that drives the local economy.

Crooked River Lighthouse—near Carrabelle Beach. This 103-foot lighthouse was built in 1895; the grounds are open to the public.

Crooked River Lighthouse, near Carrabelle Beach.

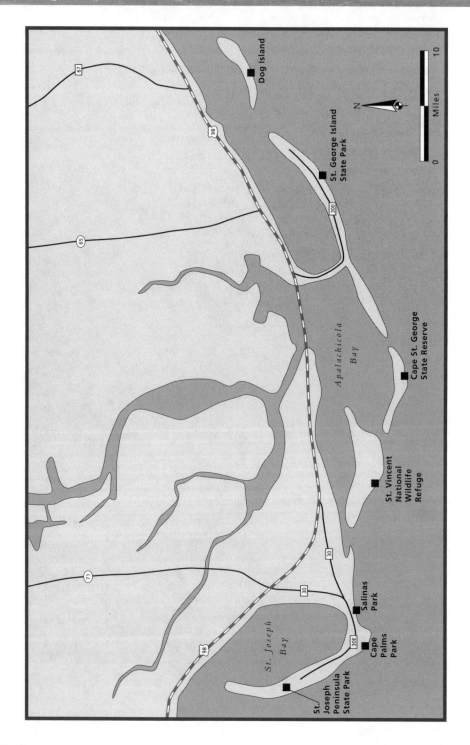

Dog Island

This offshore island is something of a curiosity due to its mixed ownership. In 1980 the Nature Conservancy bought much of the island to preserve it, though about a third of it is still a collection of private homes. The history of occupation by indigenous peoples dates back a long time, and a 1,200-year-old dugout canoe has been found on Dog Island. In modern times, many homeowners would prefer that the place remain undiscovered, and since the ferry service was discontinued there has been no access except by private boat and water taxi. Ferry service is expected to be restored, though.

Many of the 135 homeowners on this 7-mile island are weekenders from Tallahassee or vacationers; only about 20 people live there year-round. The Robinson Crusoes who call it home have a paradise of blinding-white beaches, lush forests, and teeming bird life. Camping on the island isn't allowed, and there's only one place to stay, the eight-unit Pelican Inn. It is a wonderful place for boat camping, though, and truly one of the most gorgeous spots in the state. Please take care to pack out everything you bring to the island, because it's a very fragile ecosystem.

On the mainland the 103-foot-high Crooked River Lighthouse is currently undergoing renovation. Storms and erosion take a hard toll on lighthouses around here, and no trace remains of the previous lighthouse that used to be 60 feet offshore.

ACCESS: Boat only, or by charter plane from Tallahassee. By sea kayak, you can use the car park on your left at Carrabelle Beach on US 98 on the west side of town of Carrabelle. It's a 4.5-mile paddle to the west tip of the island. Carrabelle is 55 miles south of Tallahassee on SR 319.

PARKING: Pull your boat up to the beach in the Conservancy-owned section; there's a free car park at Carrabelle Beach for kayak departures, and free parking in Carrabelle for water taxis.

HOURS/FEES: Sunrise–sunset; water taxis from Carrabelle cost $60–75 each way for up to six people. Free day use of the beach.

AMENITIES: None.

ACTIVITIES: Sunbathing, swimming, primitive camping.

FOR MORE INFORMATION: Nature Conservancy—Northwest Florida Chapter (850) 643-2756.
Sea kayak trip info www.PaddleNorthFlorida.com.

St. George Island State Park

This island contains some of the most beautiful white-sand beaches in Florida, along 8 miles of pristine coastline. Four miles of beach are accessed along the park's main road; the final 4 miles of wilderness beach are accessible only on foot. The beaches of St. George are famous for their windswept, natural state, as well as the shockingly white, powdery sand that you only find in the Panhandle. Canoes and kayaks are a fine way to mosey around the shallow bays of St. George, and can be rented in the park. Boat ramps also give access to Apalachicola Bay.

There's a full-facility campground in the pine woods, and primitive camping is allowed at the end of the 2.5-mile nature trail out to Gap Point. There are no lifeguards at the beaches, but showers are located at two of the beach accesses. The island consistently gets ranked as one of the top beaches in the United States, and for good reason. A trip to St. George is not easily forgotten.

ACCESS: From the east side of the bridge to Apalachicola on US 98, follow signs to the SR 300 bridge south to St. George Island. Turn left onto Gulf Drive and continue 4 miles to the park.

PARKING: Parking lots.

HOURS/FEES: 8:00 A.M.–sunset; $1.00 per hiker or biker, $2.00 per single-passenger vehicle, $4.00 per vehicle with two to eight passengers.

AMENITIES: Rest rooms, showers, picnic shelters, grills, campground, boat ramps, nature trails.

ACTIVITIES: Beach walking, boating, sunbathing, swimming, camping, hiking, fishing.

FOR MORE INFORMATION: St. George Island State Park (850) 927–2111. Apalachicola Bay Chamber of Commerce (850) 653–9419.

Cape St. George, also known as Little St. George Island, used to be part of a 28-mile greater island until a human-made shipping channel split it off in 1954. Now the 10 miles of pristine white-powder beaches can only be reached by boat. For those who are taken by the beauty of the wilderness beaches of St. George, this is more of the same and then some. Kayakers and canoeists can easily reach the cape by launching from St. George Island. If the wind or seas are up, it's safest to navigate the protected waters of the bay; or you can paddle the outside waters on calm days. Water taxis are available from Lafayette Park Pier in Apalachicola.

There are pine woods in the lowlands, maritime hammocks in the higher elevations. The pines were the source of turpentine in the first half of the twentieth century, and scars can still be seen on some of the pines from the process. A face of the pine was exposed so the turpentine would bleed out and could be collected. Until technology allowed chemical solvents to be produced more cheaply, "turpentine gangs" were an integral part of early Florida culture. The buildings from the camps still exist at Government Dock.

Primitive camping is allowed at a few different areas on the island, including Sikes Cut, West Pass, and Government Dock. The old Cape St. George Lighthouse is still intact, though the ocean comes ever closer to it. After two lighthouses were built and abandoned in the early nineteenth century, the present one was built 400 yards inland. Erosion has erased most of that distance.

ACCESS: By boat from Apalachicola or St. George Island State Park.

PARKING: Boat dock, car parking for departures at state park boat ramps.

HOURS/FEES: Twenty-four hours; free.

AMENITIES: Rest rooms, picnic shelter, dock, lighthouse.

ACTIVITIES: Beach walking, boating, sunbathing, swimming, primitive camping, fishing, bird-watching.

FOR MORE INFORMATION: Cape St. George State Reserve (850) 927–2111.

Apalachicola Bay Chamber of Commerce (850) 653–9419.

The group of islands that lie off of Apalachicola fall into the categories of wild, wilder, and wildest. St. Vincent would be at the wildest end of the spectrum. A national wildlife refuge that was bought by the Nature Conservancy in 1968 and donated to the federal government, the island has a curious history. (See "Never Cry Wolf," page 99.) The 9 miles of beaches feature the same waving white dunes as its neighbors, and the 4-mile-wide island is interconnected by a series of old sand roads.

Because of its width, St. Vincent has a broader ecosystem than the St. George islands, with freshwater lakes and a wide range of habitat. A short distance across Indian Pass on Cape San Blas, Tom Brocato runs an eco-tourism business called Broke-a-Toe, leading kayak tours around St. Vincent. He also runs boat shuttles over to drop off and pick up people who just

The dunes at St. Vincent National Wildlife Refuge.

want to spend the day wiggling their toes in the island's miles of empty beaches. There are no facilities at all on St. Vincent, which is unlikely to change anytime soon. Camping is not allowed, except by hunters in two designated locations during a very limited three-day season to help control the local deer population.

ACCESS: By boat shuttle from Apalachicola; by private boat or kayak from St. George Island State Park or Indian Pass.

PARKING: Car parking for departures at state park boat ramps, but no docks on the island.

HOURS/FEES: Twenty-four hours; free use of the island, $10.00 boat shuttle for adults, $7.00 under ten years old.

AMENITIES: None.

ACTIVITIES: Beach walking, boating, sunbathing, swimming, fishing, bird-watching.

FOR MORE INFORMATION: St. Vincent National Wildlife Refuge (850) 653–8808.

Broke-a-Toe kayak rentals at Indian Pass (850) 229–WAVE.

Boat shuttle operators: Apalachicola Bay Chamber of Commerce (850) 653–9419.

St. Vincent NWR.

Salinas Park

Because it's closer to the mainland than the beaches out on the exposed reaches of Cape San Blas, the sand at Salinas Park is affected by the sediment of the Apalachicola River and isn't as white as the barrier island sands of the region. It still features substantial dunes, and the large gazebo in the complex is located atop the highest dune. The fishing and shelling are quite good here, especially the latter. Picnic facilities, rest rooms, and showers make it a nice family destination, especially because of its easy access. Much of the park is nestled in pine flatwoods, which offer plenty of nearby shade to retreat to from the beach and make for nice barbecue spots.

ACCESS: From the west on US 98/SR 30, go through Port St. Joe, fork right onto SR 30A for 6 miles, turn right onto SR 30E, and go 0.5 mile to the entrance on your left.

From the east on US 98/SR 30, drive 4 miles outside Apalachicola, fork left onto SR 30A for 9 miles, turn left onto SR 30E, and go 0.5 mile to the entrance on your left.

PARKING: Parking lots.

HOURS/FEES: Sunrise–sunset, free.

AMENITIES: Rest rooms, showers, gazebo, playground, picnic areas, boardwalk.

ACTIVITIES: Sunbathing, fishing, shelling, picnicking.

FOR MORE INFORMATION: Gulf County Parks (850) 229–8944.

Salinas Park.

Cape Palms Park

Lest everything seem like a state or federal facility in this region, Gulf County has created a couple of nice beach parks with Salinas Beach and the lovely Cape Palms Park farther out on Cape San Blas. Situated amid the developed area of the cape, it doesn't have the natural dunes and splendor of the state park to the north, but it does have the spectacular white sand the region is known for. Not only that, but it also has full facilities and is free to the public. This has made it one of the favorite destinations of day-trippers in this part of the Panhandle. The park is quite new—it was constructed in 1998—so the rest rooms, playground, and picnic areas are in great shape, and the landscaping contributes to its idyllic quality. A nice boardwalk passes through dense native foliage to the beach.

Cape Palms Park.

The Cape San Blas Lighthouse isn't far south of the park, and the light has managed to stay in one place for eighty years on this erosion-ravaged coast. The previous three brick lighthouses of the nineteenth century were all washed away, and the underwater remains of one of them sits a half mile offshore! Even the modern one was moved around a few times before a site was chosen where it could survive. The steel skeleton tower is identical to the Sanibel Lighthouse on the lower Gulf.

ACCESS: From the west on US 98/SR 30, go through Port St. Joe, fork right onto SR 30A for 6 miles, turn right onto SR 30E, and go 4 miles to the entrance on your left.

From the east on US 98/SR 30, 4 miles outside Apalachicola, fork left onto SR 30A for 9 miles, turn left onto SR 30E, and continue 4 miles to the entrance on your left.

PARKING: Parking lots.

HOURS/FEES: Sunrise–sunset, free.

AMENITIES: Rest rooms, showers, pavilion, gazebo, picnic tables, grills, playground.

ACTIVITIES: Sunbathing, swimming, picnicking.

FOR MORE INFORMATION: Gulf County Parks (850) 229–8944.

Boardwalk to the beach.

St. Joseph Peninsula State Park

This peninsula on Cape San Blas is another one of the Florida beaches that regularly gets top rankings in the country. It is unquestionably one of the most gorgeous beaches in the state, stretching out for miles and miles of undeveloped beauty. The dune formations are arresting, sculpted by the wind into odd shapes. Acres and acres of pine flatwoods occupy the interior where the island widens, though some sections are ribbon-thin strips of sand between the Gulf and the bay.

Because of its isolation and recreational possibilities, it makes much more sense to camp or stay in a cabin here than day-trip. The cabins are a great deal, particularly after September 15 when the rate falls to $55 a night. Roughing it a bit more, the full-hookup campground has 119 sites, while for the no-frills adventurer there is wilderness hiking and primitive camping available in the 1,650-acre wilderness preserve section of the park. In autumn the hawk migration passes through here, and the park is one of the best

St. Joseph Peninsula State Park.

places in the eastern United States to observe it. Monarch butterflies all pass through in vast numbers on their way to their winter homes in Mexico. Kayaking, boating, and fishing opportunities are almost unlimited between the bay side and the open Gulf.

ACCESS: From the west on US 98/SR 30, go through Port St. Joe, fork right onto SR 30A for 6 miles, turn right onto SR 30E, and go 8.5 miles to the entrance.

From the east on US 98/SR 30, 4 miles outside Apalachicola, fork left onto SR 30A for 9 miles, turn left onto SR 30E, and go 8.5 miles to the entrance.

PARKING: Parking lots.

HOURS/FEES: Sunrise–sunset, $3.25 per vehicle.

AMENITIES: Rest rooms, showers, picnic tables, grills, campground, cabins, hiking trails, boat ramp, boat basin.

ACTIVITIES: Sunbathing, swimming, picnicking, beach walking, fishing, kayaking, boating, camping (cabins, tents, and primitive).

FOR MORE INFORMATION: St. Joseph Peninsula State Park (850) 227–1327.

Broke-a-Toe (kayak rentals) (850) 229–WAVE.

Driftwood.

Never Cry Wolf (Except Here)

While many national wildlife refuges in the federal system have been established as preservation areas for waterfowl—hence the Duck Stamp pass that grants you access—the St. Vincent National Wildlife Refuge discovered it had a much larger charter. Named by seventeenth-century missionaries, St. Vincent Island underwent a strange transformation in 1908. The previous owner, George Hatch, had bought the island for $3,000 in 1868, and his resting site remains the only marked grave on the island. The man who bought the island next, Dr. Pierce, imported $60,000 worth of African wildlife.

After timber companies largely deforested the island in the 1940s, the Loomis brothers bought it in 1948 for $140,000 to continue the game preserve tradition. They imported zebras, elands, black bucks, ring-necked pheasants, Asian jungle fowl, and bobwhite quail. While there are no more zebras or elands, sambra deer still inhabit the marshy areas of the island. Native to Southeast Asia, these elk relatives can weigh up to 700 pounds.

In 1968 the Nature Conservancy bought St. Vincent Island and passed it on to the federal government, which repaid them via Duck Stamp sales. The maintenance workers at the refuge know the island like no one else, being brothers who were born there. The father of Tommy and Robert Gay worked as caretaker for the Loomis brothers, and the Gays' island-bred ingenuity has made them indispensable to the upkeep of the refuge.

There is even a family of red wolves living on the island. The government found the island an ideal location to try reintroducing the red wolf to the southeastern United States, because of its isolation. Other attempts, such as in Great Smoky Mountains National Park, have mostly failed due to lack of prey. The most successful region has been in eastern North Carolina. The program has gone much more smoothly among the public than in the case of the gray wolves in Yellowstone, where ranchers raised such a hue and cry. In 1997 a female red wolf, born at the National Zoo, successfully bred with a male on St. Vincent Island, producing six pups. Five of them survived to join wild populations.

Mexico Beach is the western end of the Forgotten Coast, the part of the Panhandle stretching through Apalachicola to Carrabelle that development has largely ignored. The remarkable thing about the 1,200-person community is that there's not a single chain motel or chain restaurant in town. The beaches are the same wonderful white sand as elsewhere, but it's a place that time has forgotten—an unchanged old Florida town, which are quite common inland in this neck of the woods but rather rare on the prized coast. Cruising US 98 west, the next beaches are on the sprawling property of Tyndall Air Force Base, virtually unused wilderness areas that are postcard perfect. Access is generally available with a recreation permit, but be prepared to be denied when the military is under security alerts.

On both sides of the inlet that exits into the Gulf from the bays around Panama City, the state owns prime pieces of coastal real estate. If you prefer to take your own boat from St. Andrews State Park to Shell Island, or the ferry isn't running, be aware that this is a major shipping channel that also sees hovercrafts from the Naval Coastal Systems Station roaring in and out at high speed. Keep an eye out at all times.

Panama City has a large military population because of the bases, which has hampered its development to some degree because of the transience of the personnel. While there are plenty of good restaurants and the like, there aren't many cultural attractions. Panama City Beach, the community on the coast, is a booming resort town that hosts the largest spring break crowd in Florida each year. Whether they will decide as Fort Lauderdale and Daytona Beach did—that spring break madness is a little too much for them remains to be seen. Getting out west toward the county line, the coast gives way to pine woods and low-key development again. Secluded beaches like Camp Helen State Park begin cropping up.

Access

If you're already on US 98, cruising east from Destin and west from Port St. Joe takes you through the region.

From the north/east, take exit 19 off I–10 and head south on US 231 to Panama City, then east on US 98 to Mexico Beach.

From the north/west, from exit 15 off I–10, go south on SR 81 to SR 20 east, then south on SR 79 to US 98.

Beaches

Mexico Beach
Crooked Island East—Tyndall Air Force Base
Crooked Island West—Tyndall Air Force Base
St. Andrews State Park and Shell Island
Bay County Pier
City Pier—Panama City Beach
Camp Helen State Park

Camping

St. Andrews State Park—(850) 233–5140. Two campground loops are situated in the pine woods near Grand Lagoon. There are 176 family campsites with electricity, water, picnic tables, and grills or fire rings. The sites will accommodate camping units ranging in size from tents to rigs up to 40 feet in length. Located in the campground are two dump stations for sewage disposal. From March through September the basic rate is $17; from October through February, $10. Add $2.00 for electric and $2.00 for bayside sites.

Rustic Sands Resort Campground—(850) 648–5229, in Mexico Beach. Located on twenty acres of quiet pine grove and a short half-mile walk or drive to beach. Modern rest rooms and showers, laundry room, heated pool, recreation hall, children's playground and fishing pond, convenience store, book exchange, and modem hookup for Internet users. Seventy-five RV sites with full hookups.

Panama City Beach KOA—(850) 234–5731, 8800 Thomas Drive, Panama City Beach. Three hundred yards to the Gulf of Mexico and white sandy beaches. Adjacent to golf, restaurants, fishing, animal parks, and amusement parks. A tent site for two people costs $16–26.

Pine Log State Forest—(850) 747–5639, 715 West 15th Street, Panama City. Leashed pets allowed. Full-facility camping, primitive camping, showers, swimming, fishing, boat ramp, picnicking, hiking and nature trails, biking, equestrian trails and horseback riding. Twenty campsites, fully equipped with

electric and water hookups. Rest rooms with showers and a sanitary dump-
ing station are located on the site. Rates are $12.00 per night; senior citizens
$7.00.

Other Points of Interest

Gulf World Aquarium—(850) 234–5271, 15412 Front Beach Road, Panama
City Beach. Sea lions, seals, dolphins, and other aquatic animals.

Econfina Creek—North of Panama City on US 231. Perhaps the most
beautiful canoeing experience in Florida. Wild and remote, the upper section
is a fast, winding creek with high limestone walls. The lower section has
dozens of beautiful springs just off the river.

Panama City Beach Visitors Center—(800) PC–BEACH (722–3224). One
block from the County Pier, this is a good place to find information on diving, boat charters, hotels, and more.

Panama City Beach.

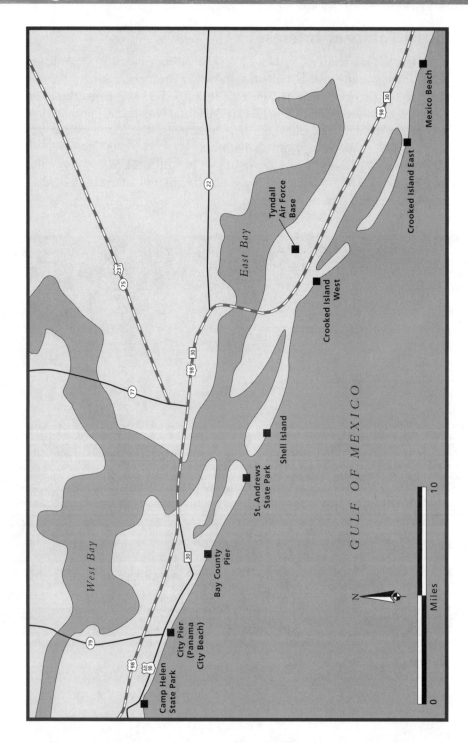

Camp Helen State Park

City Pier (Panama City Beach)

Bay County Pier

St. Andrews State Park

Shell Island

Crooked Island West

Crooked Island East

Mexico Beach

Tyndall Air Force Base

West Bay

East Bay

GULF OF MEXICO

N

Miles

0   10

Mexico Beach

Traveling along US 98 between Panama City and Port St. Joe, you come across a small fishing town called Mexico Beach. In the center of town is an old wooden pier that occasionally has waves worth surfing, and is also a popular fishing spot. At the west end of town is Canal Park, which starts by the marina and runs along the canal's edge out to the inlet. There's a nice beach here by the west jetty. At the east end of town is a boardwalk that runs along the beach.

The locals treasure the quietness and prefer their beaches to the more "glamorous" ones of the western Panhandle. An MSNBC reporter doing a story on Gulf beaches recalled her mother-in-law issuing her opinion of Destin beaches from within the Mexico Beach living room she had lived in for twenty years: "I've never been there," she harrumphed. "I don't plan to go."

ACCESS: From US 98, Canal Park and Marina is on the west side of the bridge on the west side of Mexico Beach; turn south to get to the beach portion. For the pier, turn south onto 37th Street in the center of town. Additional facilities at 7th and 19th Streets.

Fishing pier at Mexico Beach.

PARKING: Parking lots.

HOURS/FEES: Sunrise–sunset, free.

AMENITIES: Rest rooms, showers, picnic tables, pier, boardwalks, marina.

ACTIVITIES: Sunbathing, swimming, fishing, boating, picnicking.

FOR MORE INFORMATION: Canal Park (850) 648–5700.

Crooked Island East—Tyndall Air Force Base

The beaches of Tyndall Air Force Base are without question one of the best-kept secrets in the state. The base claims 18 miles of pristine white-sand beaches, vast expanses of sand, sea oats, and dunes that rarely see humans. From where the vegetation begins on the dunes, acres of wildflowers dot the landscape. Tyndall doesn't go out of its way to advertise the beaches. Their wildlife biologists prefer studying one of the rare examples of untrammeled Florida Gulf coastline, home to rare beach mice and countless other creatures, without worrying about humans doing any harm to the environment. For security reasons, too, the base would rather keep civilian access severely restricted.

In light of this, it's surprising and wonderful to know that most of the beaches are available for civilian use, if not easily accessible. At the east end of Tyndall's property lies the peninsula of Crooked Island East, which is accessed by a marked dirt road off US 98 that you can follow all the way to the beach.

There are rest rooms and showers at the beach, and 5 miles of glorious seclusion to enjoy as you wander to the west toward Crooked Island Pass. The only thing required of the few privy to this natural wonder is a recreational pass, which can be obtained at the base's Natural Resources Center. Boaters are welcome to pull up to the beach anywhere along Tyndall's shoreline, if they have a pass. Though the pass requirement seems to discourage most people, it's easy to obtain and is good for an entire year.

ACCESS: From US 98, on the east side of the DuPont Bridge to and from Panama City, turn onto Sabre Drive and continue to the gate of Tyndall Air Force Base. Obtain a gate pass at the visitor center beside the gate. Ask for directions to the Natural Resource Center. Obtain a recreation pass—which is good for a year—at the NRC, for which you'll need photo ID, vehicle registration, and proof of insurance. Go back out to US 98 and head east to just before the boundaries of the base. You'll see an unmarked road on your right; follow this out to the beach.

PARKING: Parking lot.

HOURS/FEES: Sunrise–sunset; free.

AMENITIES: Rest rooms, showers.

ACTIVITIES: Beach walking, sunbathing, swimming, fishing, picnicking.

FOR MORE INFORMATION: Tyndall Air Force Base Natural Resources Center (850) 283–2641.

Crooked Island East.

Crooked Island West—Tyndall Air Force Base

Shifting sands and storms have changed the landscape here dramatically in the past decade, and the island known alternately as Crooked Island West and Hurricane Island is now just a peninsula. Where it previously was separated from Shell Island by a pass, it has now joined its western neighbor; they look like a pair of Siamese twin peninsulas joined to the common body of the mainland. Where they meet is where Tyndall Beach of the Tyndall Air Force Base is located. This allows beach walkers the stunning options of 5 miles in one direction on Crooked Island West and 5 miles in the other direction on Shell Island. Alternately, the area can be accessed by people taking the Shell Island ferry and walking east on Shell Island. Like anywhere on Tyndall property, though, you need a recreation pass from the Natural Resources Center.

A half-mile-long boardwalk leads out from the parking lot at Tyndall Beach, crossing beautiful acres of sea oats and wildflowers. Though 5,000 people live on the base, few of them take advantage of the paradise. At the most crowded time of year, on the Fourth of July, you'll be lucky to find more than three dozen people at the beach.

ACCESS: From US 98, on the east side of the DuPont Bridge to and from Panama City, turn onto Sabre Drive and continue to the gate of Tyndall Air Force Base. Obtain a gate pass at the visitor center beside the gate. Ask for directions to the Natural Resource Center. Obtain a recreation pass—which is good for a year—at the NRC, for which you'll need photo ID, vehicle registration, and proof of insurance. Ask for directions to Tyndall Beach. A half-mile board-walk runs from the parking area.

PARKING: Parking lot.

HOURS/FEES: Sunrise–sunset; free.

AMENITIES: Rest rooms, showers, boardwalk.

ACTIVITIES: Beach walking, sunbathing, swimming, fishing, picnicking.

FOR MORE INFORMATION: Tyndall Air Force Base Natural Resources Center (850) 283–2641.

Depending on how one or another has been affected by storms, St. Andrews trades off with St. Joseph and St. George to the east as one of the top ten beaches in the country each year. Located a few miles east of the craziness of Panama City Beach, St. Andrews is a peaceful haven for the Panama City residents who aren't up to facing the strip that spring break made famous. The idyllic state park of more than a 1,000 acres is a combination of woodlands, marshes, and beach, with nature trails, fishing piers, and boat ramps giving you access to every inch of it. Overnight camping is available in the large campground.

The park has been around for a half century, opening soon after it was decommissioned as a military base. Cannon platforms near the jetties are a

Shell Island.

favorite perch to watch sunsets from. A reconstructed turpentine still is the starting point for one of the nature trails, which winds around through the pine woods and marshes, where you can see alligators and wading birds.

The waters are often strikingly clear around here, even more so across the channel at Shell Island. A ferry runs in spring and summer over to the island, and the concession offers snorkeling packages and kayak rentals as well. Shell Island runs all the way east into Tyndall Air Force Base property and is an undeveloped paradise. Bottlenose dolphins play here by the dozens—this concentration of Florida's favorite sea mammal is one of the greatest in the world. One of the rare pleasures for surfers in the area is when the surf spot called Amazons starts happening. Amazons is a left break that peels along the channel side of the east jetty, and when it gets a good hurricane swell, it's the best break along the entire Gulf Coast of Florida. Because you need a boat to access it, surfers often camp out at St. Andrews the night before so they can be out at the Shell Island break at first light.

ACCESS: From US 98 on the west side of Hathaway Bridge in western Panama City, take CR 3031 south for 4 miles and turn left into the park.

PARKING: Parking lots.

HOURS/FEES: 8:00 A.M.–sunset; $1.00 per hiker or biker, $2.00 per single-passenger vehicle, $4.00 per vehicle with two to eight passengers. The Shell Island ferry costs $9.50 adults, $5.50 children; infants are free.

AMENITIES: Rest rooms, showers, picnic shelter, island ferry, boat ramp, food concessions, kayak rentals, visitor center.

ACTIVITIES: Sunbathing, swimming, fishing, boating, picnicking, beach walking.

FOR MORE INFORMATION: St. Andrews State Park (850) 233–5140.

Friends of St. Andrews (850) 233–5117.

Bay County Pier

This is the happening hub of beach life in the Panama City Beach area. When locals talk about "PCB," rest assured, they're not talking about a toxic chemical that inhabits the area, just the abbreviated name for the beach town. Though the infamous carnival it has become during spring break is well known, it's a year-round destination for the young and the buff. While there's more breathtaking wilderness beach in this region of the Gulf than seems fair, there aren't too many all-purpose party beaches for the young crowd. This is one of the hot spots. As one local newspaper writer noted, there are more people in the bathrooms here on any given weekend than on the entire beach at Tyndall Air Force Base.

Beach divers.

The pier is a fine fishing spot, and also popular with surfers. The beach is very child friendly, with a play area in the county park as well as summer lifeguards. During the rest of the year the overtaxed beach patrol cruises back and forth on ATVs, trying to cover miles of beach on a moving basis. Thankfully, during spring break the water is far too cold for most people to want to swim.

ACCESS: From US 98 on the west side of the Hathaway Bridge in western Panama City, take CR 3031 south for 4 miles, then turn left into the parking lot.

PARKING: Parking lots.

HOURS/FEES: Sunrise–sunset; free.

AMENITIES: Summer lifeguards, rest rooms, showers, pavilion, picnic tables, pier, playground.

ACTIVITIES: Sunbathing, swimming, fishing, picnicking, children's play.

FOR MORE INFORMATION: Bay County Parks (850) 784–4066.

Panama City Beach Visitors Center (800) PC–BEACH (722–3224).

Bay County Chamber of Commerce (850) 785–5206.

City Pier—Panama City Beach

Owning the title of longest pier in the Gulf, the PCB City Pier is soon to become known for a lot more. The pier situation is a little confusing, because the Bay County Pier is in the heart of Panama City Beach, and the City Pier is located way out at the western end of PCB. The massive St. Joe Paper Company, one of the largest landholders in the Panhandle, has unveiled plans for Pier Park, an entertainment complex that will house a 1,500-seat Grand Ole Opry theater, a large retail village, and restaurants. One of the restaurants will be Jimmy Buffett's Margaritaville. Along with the development will come a new eighty-acre city park, with six acres of beach.

This will add to an already nice beach area that has summer lifeguards and is open twenty-four hours. Because of the great distance it juts out into the Gulf, the pier is one of the finest fishing spots in the area. It's also a good place just to walk out on, giving you panoramic views of miles of beach.

Panama City Beach pier.

ACCESS: From US 98, 6 miles west of Panama City, take SR 79 south. Turn left onto SR 30/Alternate US 98; it's 1 mile to the pier.

PARKING: Parking lots.

HOURS/FEES: Twenty-four hours; free.

AMENITIES: Summer lifeguards, rest rooms, showers, picnic tables, pier.

ACTIVITIES: Sunbathing, swimming, fishing, picnicking, children's play.

FOR MORE INFORMATION: Panama City Beach Pier (850) 233–5080.

Panama City Beach Visitor Center (800) PC–BEACH (722–3224).

Camp Helen State Park

This is one of the newest parks in the state system, one of seven in the Choctaw GeoPark system that extends west to Henderson Beach. The park is comprised of 183 acres of woodlands, mostly pine woods, as well as some of the last pristine maritime hammock in the region. An old abandoned lodge sits on the property, built by an Indiana entrepreneur who had the logs floated up from South America.

New facilities are nearly completed, and the entire park will be open in 2003. A trail leads through the woods and dunes to a beautiful, secluded beach. Some locals have been using it for a long time as a clothing-optional beach, so don't be surprised if you encounter someone in the buff. Separated only by an inlet from the west edge of Panama City Beach, this wild expanse could be another world.

ACCESS: From US 98, head 8 miles west of Panama City on the Bay County side of the Bay-Walton County line, then turn south into the park.

PARKING: Very limited parking.

HOURS/FEES: 8:00 A.M.–sunset; free.

AMENITIES: None.

ACTIVITIES: Sunbathing, beach walking, swimming, fishing.

FOR MORE INFORMATION: Camp Helen State Park (850) 231–4210.

Camp Helen State Park.

Dolphins

There are few sights at the beach as wonderful to watch as a pod of dolphins playing in the surf. Though surfers around the world are notoriously grudging about whom they share their waves with, no surfer minds when dolphins come in to catch a few. Their devotion to sheer, carefree play is an inspiration, and a reminder of just what it is we love so much about the ocean. Considered one of the most intelligent mammals in the world, next to humans—and by many standards of human behavior you could argue they're way ahead of us—dolphins are a constant source of fascination to us. Ever since Flipper became known around the world, and Miami's football team adopted them as a mascot, dolphins have been identified as part of the heart and soul of Florida.

In 1961 the Miami Seaquarium received a plea from the small Italian town of Cesenatico, which had a woeful female porpoise named Lalla. She needed a playmate, and so my grandmother came up with a promotional scheme to send the town a boy porpoise named Palooza. Her journalist friend John Keasler, along with humorist Art Buchwald, escorted Palooza to Italy. Lalla was delighted with her new boy pal, but soon found she had competition for his attentions, as evidenced by this letter to my grandmother from Cesenatico:

> Palooza is so brisk that he is flirting with Ciumba, the best friend of his wife, Lalla. To call more attention to his love evolutions, Palooza jumps very often; this is very strange, because till now Palooza, always so sluggish, seemed to fail the well-known tradition of American marines, who fascinate Italian girls, too. Unfortunately this passing rapidly from Ciumba to Lalla did not give the "fruit of the sin": of course, that's natural! For a regular procreation is necessary an honest and faithful union, and Palooza...well, he doesn't know it at all.
>
> We do hope in 1962. What will happen till then? Divorce or not divorce between Lalla and Palooza? Ciumba, Palooza's passionate lover, has all the physical requisites and Palooza seems to like her very much. All this has been observed during this summertime: sun, blue sky, moon, are the fittest ingredients to favour the most ungovernable loves. We have to acknowledge Palooza has become a really Latin lover and has lost that kind of appreciable ingenuity of American boys with their hairs cut very short.

Consequently, we advise all the American young people to come to Cesenatico, where, well... perhaps, they can also become like Palooza.

Around Shell Island near Panama City, one of the largest concentrations of bottlenose dolphins in the world makes a home. The bottlenose is the same dolphin as Flipper—*Delphinus delphis*—and the most common. *Dolphin* and *porpoise* are words often used interchangeably, though the entire family of creatures is *Delphinidae* and *porpoise* is used more accurately to describe varieties other than the bottlenose dolphin. In the ocean you encounter both the bottlenose dolphin and the spotted porpoise, the latter being considerably smaller and more likely to be found well offshore. Interestingly, some bottlenose dolphins spend their entire lives in rivers like the Indian River Lagoon on the east coast of Florida, while others come and go from the ocean at will. Regardless of where they choose to live, they always bring a smile to my face, and the desire that we all could be so exuberant.

The beaches of southern Walton County are plentiful, and they're part of the Panhandle that can be classified as discovered but not overrun. The rush of development in recent years began in a modest, residential fashion, with communities like Seaside that attempted to re-create old-time neighborhoods and quieter times. Most of the film *The Truman Show*, which was a sort of comic nightmare about the manipulation of a living environment, was filmed here. Celebrities came to Seaside for vacations, and it became the blueprint for other developments in south Walton. Unfortunately Seaside and many of the other communities have grown past the original vision, densely packing in as many homes as possible. Sections of the coastal highway have been essentially privatized to resemble slow roads in gated communities and driving through these areas can be a chore. In the midst of all these model communities is one of the oldest coastal towns in the region, Grayton Beach, which remains a funky blend of old Florida characteristics.

The coastal road that links all these communities together is CR 30A, which features an 18-mile bike path. Towns prefer not to advertise their public beach access to outsiders, however, and you have to look hard in Inlet Beach, for example, to find the beach parking areas. Oh, but the beaches! They all share that same extraordinary combination of colors: dazzling white against emerald green and turquoise. Lest this get repetitious, the state parks provide nature trails through the woods, lake fishing, and other activities. The state park beaches are staggering in their beauty, and Grayton Beach State Recreation Area is especially so. With boardwalks leading through rolling, untouched dunes, the state beaches are unparalleled in their expansiveness.

Crossing into Okaloosa County as you approach Destin, the quality of the built environment changes and gets increasingly dense. Though Destin sells itself on the Emerald Coast reputation, few of these beaches can actually be claimed by Destin. Developers got a little overeager in the 1980s, and by the time everyone took a breath and looked around, all the waterfront had been built up. Still, the county beaches just east of Destin, along with the state park at Henderson Beach, are as beautiful as can be. If you have any interest in deep-sea fishing, this is one of the things Destin is most famous for. Numerous charter boats run out of Destin Pass to the deep offshore waters of the Gulf, and record-size marlin have been caught out of here. There's even a fishing museum celebrating the town's connection with the sea.

Access

From the east—West on US 98 from Panama City to CR 30A.

From the west—East on US 98 from Fort Walton Beach into Destin.

From the north—Take exit 14 off I–10, then south on US 331 to US 98.

Beaches

Inlet Beach
Deer Lake State Park
Grayton Beach State Park
Blue Mountain Beach
Ed Walline Park
Fort Panic Park
Topsail Hill State Preserve
James Lee County Park
Henderson Beach State Park

Camping

Grayton Beach State Park—(850) 231–4210. Thirty-seven campsites in pine scrub near Western Lake are equipped with picnic tables, grills, water, and electricity. Park rangers provide campfire programs seasonally. Fees run $8.00–10.00 from October through February, $14.00–17.00 from March through September. Fully furnished cabins from October through February are $85 a night; from March through September, $160 a night. Ten cabins are available, with twenty more to follow soon.

Topsail Hill State Preserve RV Resort—(850) 267–0299. RV camping is provided in 156 campsites with full hookups. Concrete pads, concrete patios, with picnic tables. Cable television and telephone hookups are available. Pets are allowed with restrictions. There are twelve bungalows in a small neighborhood setting with beautifully landscaped lawns and the natural setting of the preserve out the back door. Each bungalow has a carport, full kitchen, bathroom, bedroom, and living room. All are completely furnished. Rentals run from one to six months.

Henderson Beach State Park—(850) 837–7550. A full-facility 208-acre park with showers, campsites, picnicking, pavilion, swimming, surf fishing, and

Topsail Hill State Preserve.

more than 6,000 feet of scenic Gulf-front shoreline. Thirty campsites with electric and water hookups are available; $16–18 per night.

Other Points of Interest

Eden State Gardens and Mansion—(850) 231–4214, CR 395, Point Washington. A restored 1895 house in Greek Revival style with Louis XV and Louis XVI period furniture. Gardens of live oaks dripping Spanish moss, with azaleas and camellias. Open Thursday through Monday.

CR30A Scenic Bike Trail—Eighteen miles of trail from Inlet Beach to Dune Allen Beach.

Old Destin Post Office—(850) 837–8572, on Stahlman Avenue in Destin. Artifacts, photos, historic objects and data reflect the culture of early Destin pioneers. Destin's first post office was set up in a home parlor in 1897. Open Wednesday 1:30–4:30 P.M.

The Destin Fishing Museum—(850) 654–1011, Moreno Plaza, 35 US 98 East, Destin. A collection of memorabilia and artifacts celebrating the history of deep-sea fishing.

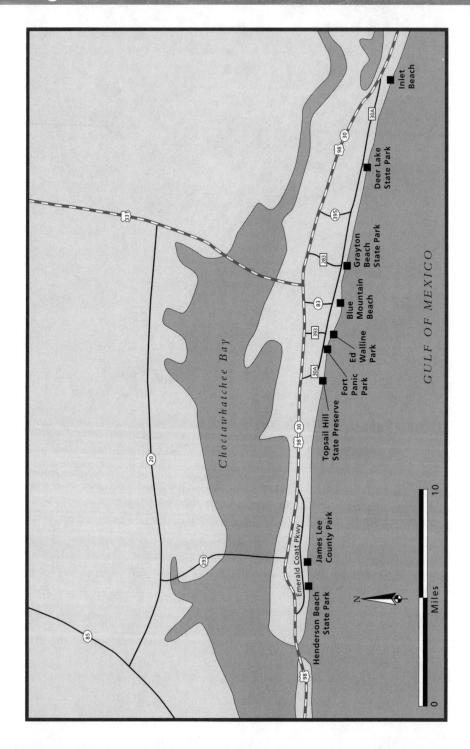

Inlet Beach

30A

98 30

Deer Lake State Park

395

Grayton Beach State Park

283

Blue Mountain Beach

83

393

Ed Walline Park

30A

Fort Panic Park

30

Topsail Hill State Preserve

331

98 30

Choctawhatchee Bay

20

293

Emerald Coast Pkwy

James Lee County Park

65

Henderson Beach State Park

98

GULF OF MEXICO

N

Miles

0   10

Inlet Beach

This pleasant beach is the beginning of the CR 30A Scenic Bike Trail, a beautiful 18-mile stretch of coastal biking that links a number of great beaches and facilities. There are basic shower and rest room facilities; otherwise it's just sun, sand, and the Gulf of Mexico, which morphs from emerald close to shore to deep blue as the water deepens. The beach access is a spacious nineteen-acre park, and the community is named after the lagoon on its eastern shore, Philips Inlet.

> **ACCESS:** From US 98, go to the community of Inlet Beach 10 miles west of Panama City Beach. Turn west onto CR 30A and the beach is on your left at the Rosemary Beach border.
>
> **PARKING:** Parking lot.
>
> **HOURS/FEES:** Sunrise–sunset; free.
>
> **AMENITIES:** Rest rooms, showers, picnic shelters.
>
> **ACTIVITIES:** Sunbathing, swimming, picnicking.
>
> **FOR MORE INFORMATION:** South Walton Tourist Development Council Beach Services (800) 822–6877 or (850) 267–1216; www.BeachesofSouthWalton.com.

Deer Lake State Park

Another one of the Choctaw GeoParks, Deer Lake opened at the same time as Camp Helen in 1997. The parks are similar, though Deer Lake is ten times the size of Camp Helen, encompassing vast sections of pine woods. It is also a free park with limited facilities and parking, and has an idyllic beach. You'll find the occasional nude bather here as well, though it's not legal in the county. Not enough people use the area for anyone to mind, it seems, and enforcement is pretty much nonexistent. With picnic tables in the woods, it's a great place to take the time for a quiet lunch, even if you're just passing through. About 5 miles north on SR 395 is Eden State Gardens, home of a restored 1895 mansion and gardens of azaleas, camellias, and live oaks.

ACCESS: From the west on US 98, 18 miles east of Destin, turn right onto SR 395. Drive 4 miles south to the beach and turn left onto CR 30A; it's 2.5 miles to the park.

From the east on US 98, fork left onto CR 30A at Inlet Beach and go 8 miles to just before the town of Seagrove Beach.

PARKING: Very limited parking.

HOURS/FEES: 8:00 A.M.–sunset; free.

AMENITIES: Rest rooms, picnic tables.

ACTIVITIES: Sunbathing, swimming, picnicking, unofficial nude beach.

FOR MORE INFORMATION: Deer Lake State Park c/o Grayton Beach State Park (850) 231–4210; www.BeachesofSouthWalton.com.

Eden State Gardens (850) 231–4214.

Grayton Beach State Park

Located next to one of the oldest coastal communities in Walton County, Grayton Beach State Park is a beautiful 2,000-acre chunk of forest and beach. Sand gets blown around so much on the dunes that the shrubs you see from a distance turn out to be full-grown southern magnolias and slash pines that have been mostly buried under mounds of sand. A nature trail starts at the beach and twists through the sand dunes and woods, and there's a small campground on the shores of Western Lake. The lake is a long expanse of nooks, threads, and crannies, with salt marshes surrounding it. There's a boat ramp; good fishing is available throughout.

The beach runs on for a full mile with a picnic pavilion overlooking the water, and the water usually stays pleasant through November. The community of Grayton Beach has been described as the Key West of North Florida. The locals are a diverse mix of old residents, artists, and young professionals; there are some great funky bars and seafood restaurants. Recently the park added luxury cabins, with ten nestled in the woods and more to come. Paved bike trails lead to town from the cabins. In the off season—October through February—they're a good deal at $85 a night. Each 800-square-foot cabin is furnished with two bedrooms, a bathroom, a full kitchen, and a gas fireplace, along with a screened-in back porch.

Grayton Beach.

ACCESS: From US 98, midway between Destin and Panama City, take CR 283 south for 3 miles.

PARKING: Parking lots.

HOURS/FEES: 8:00 A.M.–sunset; $3.25 per vehicle.

AMENITIES: Rest rooms, showers, campground, cabins, picnic shelters, boat ramp, nature trails.

ACTIVITIES: Sunbathing, swimming, fishing, boating, hiking, picnicking.

FOR MORE INFORMATION: Grayton Beach State Park (850) 231–4210.

Blue Mountain Beach

This is another one of the tiny county beaches that pop up sporadically along the scenic coastal road. There are only twelve parking spaces, but if you can get one of them it's quite an interesting place. The name of the little village comes from it being the highest on the Gulf of Mexico within the United States. It is thought that the name came from the abundance of the stunning blue Gulf Coast lupines that sailors first observed on the dunes here. A veritable cliff face overlooks the water, and a boardwalk and stairs lead down to the beach.

Not so long ago, laments the surf guide *Swell.com*, "The curving scenic road, bordered by coastal lakes, had no stop signs, and you could drive 90 miles an hour and see the beach along the way. It was widely known that there was only one police car in South Walton County, and he was usually at the station, drinking coffee." The increase in development of the area has slowed the traffic down, which is to the benefit of anyone except Fort Walton Beach surfers hellbent for Panama City. Every one of these beaches along the Emerald Coast is a dreamy blend of bright white sand and crystal-clear water.

ACCESS: From US 98, 15 miles east of Destin, turn south onto SR 83 and continue 3 miles south to the beach.

From CR 30A, go to the town of Blue Mountain Beach, 16 miles east of Destin; the beach is 6 miles east of CR 30A's junction with US 98.

PARKING: Parking lot, twelve spaces.

HOURS/FEES: Twenty-four hours; free.

AMENITIES: Rest rooms, picnic tables, showers, gazebo.

ACTIVITIES: Sunbathing, swimming, picnicking.

FOR MORE INFORMATION: South Walton TDC Beach Services (850) 267–1216 or (800) 822–6877; www.BeachesofSouthWalton.com.

Even without the glut of secluded state park beaches in the region, Walton County would have plenty enough of its own parks to be proud of. Ed Walline Park has more of the powdery white sand that blinds your eyes and delights your toes. A boardwalk leads down to the beach, and the shallow water is great for frolicking and swimming. Though there are no lifeguards, the water stays shallow for so far from shore that it's hard to get in trouble. For most of the year the water is gloriously clear, the blue appearing more green from the beach because of the peculiar reflective qualities of the white Appalachian quartz sand. There's a quirky and comfortable cafe across the street, which is a good place to get coffee and pastries.

ACCESS: From US 98, 13 miles east of Destin, turn south onto CR 393; it's 3 miles south to the beach.

From CR 30A head to the town of Santa Rosa Beach, 13 miles east of Destin; 4 miles east of the CR 30A junction with US 98, look for the beach at junction of CR 30A and CR 393.

Sand Castle

PARKING: Parking lot.

HOURS/FEES: Twenty-four hours; free.

AMENITIES: Rest rooms, picnic tables, showers, boardwalk.

ACTIVITIES: Sunbathing, swimming, picnicking.

FOR MORE INFORMATION: South Walton Tourist Development Council Beach Services (850) 267–1216 or (800) 822–6877; www.BeachesofSouthWalton.com.

Fort Panic Park

Fort Panic is the last of the string of small county beaches along CR 30A, with the same amenities and glorious beach as the others. It is just a 0.5 mile west of Ed Walline Park, within the town of Dune Allen Beach, which is the end of the 18-mile scenic bike trail that runs along the coast from Inlet Beach to the east. Toward the end of a ride, there's nothing more refreshing than jumping in the lovely Gulf waters and having a nice freshwater shower afterward. Like the other facilities, it is open twenty-four hours and free to use, which allows you to happily pull up and watch sunrises or sunsets. Though there's a certain uniformity to most of the county beaches, it is a picture-postcard perfection that you can't argue about copying.

ACCESS: From the west on US 98, 11 miles east of Destin, fork right onto CR 30A and head 3 miles east to the beach.

From the east on US 98, turn left onto CR 393 and drive south 3 miles, then turn right onto CR 30A and go 1.3 miles to the beach.

PARKING: Parking lot.

HOURS/FEES: Twenty-four hours; free.

AMENITIES: Rest rooms, picnic tables, showers.

ACTIVITIES: Sunbathing, swimming, picnicking.

FOR MORE INFORMATION: South Walton TDC Beach Services (850) 267–1216 or (800) 822–6877; www.BeachesofSouthWalton.com.

Topsail Hill State Preserve

The sprawling state park of Topsail Hill derives its name from the 25-foot-high sand dune that tops the area. This is one of the largest public beaches on the Emerald Coast, extending for 3.5 miles. Lined by the shimmering Gulf on one side and high dunes on the other, this stretch of white sand boggles the mind. The 1,640-acre park reaches inland all the way to the junction of US 98 and CR 30A, encompassing lakes, pine woods, and maritime hammock. East of Tyndall Air Force Base, it's one of the few locations where rare beach mice thrive. Nature trails wind through the woods, and a boardwalk leads to the beach.

One of the other things that makes Topsail Hill unique is it's the only state park to feature an RV resort. The state bought up an RV resort in 1998 and took over the operation of it, with 156 campsites with full hookups available. In addition, there are twelve furnished bungalows that can be rented for one to six months. Two miles of pavement in the resort give you lots of room to in-line skate and bike, and there's everything from a clubhouse to a country store. For people looking to spend a long vacation or part of the winter at one of the most beautiful locations in the state, this is hard to beat.

ACCESS: From US 98, 11 miles east of Destin, turn onto CR 30A and go east for 0.25 mile to the preserve entrance.

PARKING: Parking lot.

HOURS/FEES: Sunrise–sunset; free.

AMENITIES: Rest rooms, picnic tables, showers, RV resort, cabins, nature trails, boardwalk, country store.

ACTIVITIES: Sunbathing, swimming, picnicking, fishing, snorkeling, in-line skating, bicycling, beach walking.

FOR MORE INFORMATION: Topsail Hill State Preserve (877) 232–2478.

James Lee County Park

A county beach on the edge of Destin, this is a public-private venture where a restaurant on the beach takes the place of the traditional—and not often that good—food concession you find at public beaches. The restaurant is called the Crab Trap, and is a reasonably priced and decent seafood venue. By now you're getting hemmed in by the condos of Destin, so there's not the pristine expanse you find farther east, but it's still a good family beach with volleyball and picnic areas. Because it's one of the only beaches in Destin that's open late—Henderson shuts at sundown—it's a favorite spot for people to gather to watch the sunset.

ACCESS: From the west on US 98, just east of Destin, fork right onto Emerald Coast Parkway and continue 4 miles to the park, on the Okaloosa side of the county line.

James Lee County Park.

From the east on US 98, just west of Sandestin, fork left onto Emerald Coast Parkway and continue 2.5 miles to the park, just inside the Okaloosa County line.

PARKING: Parking lot.

HOURS/FEES: 6:00 A.M.–9:00 P.M.; free.

AMENITIES: Rest rooms, picnic pavilion, showers, restaurant.

ACTIVITIES: Volleyball, sunbathing, swimming, dining, surfing.

FOR MORE INFORMATION: Emerald Coast Visitor Bureau (850) 651–7131.

Henderson Beach State Park

One of the few parcels that survived the boom in Destin was Henderson Beach, which the Henderson family sold to the state in 1983 to ensure its preservation. It's like a scaled-down version of Topsail Hill Preserve to the east. More than a mile of uncluttered beach edges on the Gulf, backed by woods full of sand pines, scrub oaks, and southern magnolias. Boardwalks run across the dunes, where sea oats and wildflowers flourish. A small campground with thirty sites offers a secluded, proletarian alternative to the hotels and resorts of the nearby bustle.

ACCESS: From the west on US 98, just east of Destin, fork right onto Emerald Coast Parkway. It's 2 miles to the park.

From the east on US 98, just west of Sandestin, fork left onto Emerald Coast Parkway. It's 4 miles to the park.

PARKING: Parking lot.

HOURS/FEES: 8:00 A.M.–sunset; $2.00 per vehicle.

AMENITIES: Rest rooms, picnic pavilion, showers, boardwalks, hiking trails, campground.

ACTIVITIES: Beach walking, sunbathing, swimming, camping, fishing, nature viewing, picnicking.

FOR MORE INFORMATION: Henderson Beach State Park (850) 837–7550.

Boys in the surf at Henderson Beach.

When Is Too Little Too Much?

The variety of moral standards that govern swimwear in Florida is interesting. Unlike most other states in the nation with coastlines, Florida encompasses such a diverse array of cultures in its vast lengths of beaches that standards vary widely throughout the state. While the locals may know the score, for visitors the changes from one county to the next are often inexplicable, particularly to our European cousins to whom bare breasts are as much a part of beach life as croissants are part of breakfast. In some rural counties with substantial miles of wilderness beaches, it can seem perfectly safe to go topless, and even bottomless, when few other souls are around. This is not always true, however, especially in rural counties governed by deeply conservative values and overzealous law enforcement.

On the other hand, the Fort Lauderdale area is a booming urban center and still goes through fits and starts of banning thong bikinis from beaches, arresting topless Europeans, and randomly enforcing strict standards. In contrast, just down the road in Miami you can wear or not wear just about anything in South Beach, and at Haulover Beach they have the only official nude beach in the state. Key West is wild, though the rest of the Florida Keys are much more subdued. Where I grew up surfing, at the Hobe Sound National Wildlife Refuge, nude sunbathers were common. Occasionally there would be arrests made by the local police, prompted—rumor had it—by the matriarch of the exclusive community adjacent to the refuge. She didn't want anyone else around, so that she could sunbathe nude herself in total privacy.

Some places you can't plan for, and up-to-date local knowledge is helpful. Stop by a surf- or swimwear shop near the beach and ask if there are any restrictive ordinances on bikini size or overvigilant enforcement of exposure laws. The few places that have passed laws against thong bikinis have attracted more exposure than they've repressed, and the laws are virtually never enforced. Otherwise, discretion usually keeps you in good stead. Keep a wrap with you to cover up if necessary. Put a good distance between you and clothed bathers. And if you're questioned, reply in French.

S anta Rosa Island is the longest barrier island in the Panhandle, stretching for 40 miles from Fort Walton Beach to Pensacola. Most of the eastern half belongs to Eglin Air Force Base, with a short interruption of festive public beaches below the inland city of Fort Walton Beach. The fantastically long Okaloosa Island Pier is one of the hubs that activity revolves around. While the 3.5 miles of Eglin property on the eastern tip of Santa Rosa—between the Fort Walton beaches and Destin Pass—are open to the public, the 15 miles west of western beaches are not. The people assigned to Eglin live within a virtual paradise of recreational opportunity, but are usually too busy protecting our nation to utilize it. The rest of us can go many places in the interior of the huge Eglin base with a recreational permit, but not the western beaches.

Where the off-limits Eglin property comes to an end, the town of Navarre and its beachfront pop up. It's an unassuming little town that is the only spot of coastal development in the middle of Santa Rosa Island. The only controversy that Navarre has experienced in recent times revolves around the tradition of nudists using the secluded area of beach adjacent to Eglin.

The Gulf Islands National Seashore returns the coast to its original wilderness state, uninterrupted until the town of Pensacola Beach. This community takes up 8 miles of the island, and provides an outlet for the city of Pensacola. There are restaurants, bars, and hotels packed along here, and busy beaches full of young people, suntan lotion, and socializing. Throughout the year there are Mardi Gras celebrations, a triathlon, wine tastings, a summer music series, boat racing, and the annual Blue Angel air show in July featuring the navy's precision flying team. At the western tip of Santa Rosa, the national seashore resumes and encompasses the Fort Pickens area, which is part of the rich naval history of Pensacola. Across Pensacola Pass is the lovely barrier island of Perdido Key, which is accessed via a detour inland through Pensacola.

Access

From the north/east—Take exit 12 off I–10 and head south on SR 85 to Fort Walton Beach and US 98.

From the west—From exit 4 off I–10, go south on I–110 to downtown Pensacola. Continue on US 98 south to Santa Rosa Island, or take exit 1 to SR 292 (Barrancas Avenue) south to Perdido Key.

Beaches

Eglin Air Force Base
Beasley/Brackin Wayside Parks—Okaloosa Island Pier
Navarre Beach
Opal Beach—Gulf Islands National Seashore
Casino Beach
Fort Pickens Gate and East Park
Langdon Beach/Fort Pickens—Gulf Islands National Seashore
Johnson Beach—Gulf Islands National Seashore
Perdido Key State Park

Camping

Eglin Air Force Base—(850) 882–4164. Natural Resources Branch is located at 107 SR 85 North, Niceville. Twenty different backcountry locations in the interior of the inland part of Eglin property are available for primitive camping. Requires a $5.00 camping permit, which is good for five days.

Fort Pickens Campground—(800) 365–CAMP, or www.reservations.nps.gov. Located on the west end of Santa Rosa Island, south of Pensacola, in the Gulf Islands National Seashore. Two hundred campsites feature paved parking pads, picnic tables, grills, and water and electric hookups; they're located in an area that includes grass, pines, and oak trees. The Gulf of Mexico and Pensacola Bay are a short walking distance from the campground. Electric sites are $20 per night, nonelectric $15 per night. Overnight stays are limited to thirty days per calendar year, with no more than fourteen days between March 1 and Labor Day.

Johnson Beach, Gulf Islands National Seashore—(850) 455–5167. Primitive camping on the beach is free. You must hike at least a half mile from the parking area and get a permit to leave a car overnight from Fort Barrancas Visitor Center. The center is open 9:30 A.M.–4:45 P.M. from March through October, 8:30 A.M.–3:45 P.M. November through February, and is located at Pensacola Naval Air Station.

Big Lagoon State Park—(850) 492–1595. Located on Gulf Beach Highway on the mainland side across from Perdido Key. Those 678 acres of natural habitat host an array of birds, animals, and waterfowl, with more than seventy-five campsites, an amphitheater, a boat ramp and dock, a boardwalk, nature trails, and an observation tower with a spectacular view. Rates are $14–16 per night.

Other Points of Interest

Indian Temple Mound Museum and Park—(850) 243–6521, 139 Miracle Strip Parkway, Fort Walton Beach. The temple mound, located on the museum grounds, represents one of the most outstanding artifacts left by early visitors to this area. Built as a ceremonial and political center by the Mound Builder culture, this mound is the largest located on salt water and possibly one of the largest prehistoric earthworks on the Gulf Coast. Fees are $2.00 for adults, $1.00 for children ages six through seventeen; children under five are free.

Gulfarium—(850) 244–5169, 1010 Miracle Strip Parkway, Fort Walton Beach. Dolphins, penguins, sharks, sea lions, and seals.

Air Force Armament Museum—(850) 882–4062, off SR 85 near Eglin Air Force Base. The only facility in the United States dedicated to displaying air force armament. The SR-71 Blackbird, the B-52, the F-15, and a Russian MIG-21 are among the main attractions displayed at this museum. Open seven days a week, except Thanksgiving, Christmas, and New Year's. Admission is free.

Blackwater River State Park—(850) 623–2363, off US 90, 15 miles northwest of Fort Walton Beach. Canoeing, camping, hiking, and fishing.

Gulf Breeze Zoo—(850) 932–2229, 5701 Gulf Breeze Parkway, just south of Pensacola. More than 700 animals surrounded by fifty acres of botanical gardens, plus a petting zoo, aviary, train ride, and shows. At this friendly zoo, you can get a close look at bears, tigers, rhinos, and zebras, as well as lowland gorillas.

Pensacola Naval Air Station—(850) 452–3604, 1750 Radford Boulevard, Pensacola. Home of the Blue Angels. The National Museum of Naval Aviation is one of the largest and most beautiful air and space museums in the world. See more than 140 beautifully restored aircraft representing navy, marine corps, and Coast Guard aviation. Also an IMAX theater and flight simulator. Open 9:00 A.M.–5:00 P.M., admission is free. The naval air station houses the Barrancas Lighthouse, which was constructed in 1857 and is rumored to house at least three ghosts. Bring a picture ID to be admitted past the front gate.

Pensacola Museum of Art—(850) 432–6247, 407 South Jefferson Street, Pensacola. Housed in the old city jail building, the Pensacola Museum of Art hosts between fourteen and eighteen exhibitions annually as well as a variety of related programs such as lectures, workshops, and free family days. Museum store and reference library. Tuesday through Friday 10:00 A.M.–5:00 P.M., Saturday 10:00 A.M.–4:00 P.M. Adults $2.00, students and military $1.00.

Good fishing in the Panhandle.

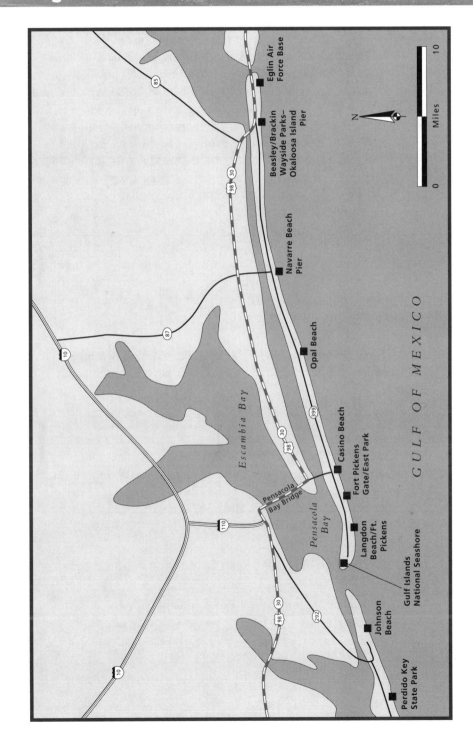

Eglin Air
Force Base

Beasley/Brackin
Wayside Parks–
Okaloosa Island
Pier

Navarre Beach
Pier

Opal Beach

N

Miles

10

0

Escambia Bay

Pensacola Bay

Casino Beach

Fort Pickens
Gate/East Park

Pensacola
Bay Bridge

Langdon
Beach/Ft.
Pickens

GULF OF MEXICO

Gulf Islands
National Seashore

Johnson
Beach

Perdido Key
State Park

Eglin Air Force Base

Like Tyndall Air Force Base, Eglin is a massive landholder in the Panhandle. In fact, the 724 square miles of land that are part of the base make it the largest air base in the democratic world. Unfortunately, not much of its coastline is open to the public. The 3.5-mile section bordering on Destin Pass on the west side is, though people hoping to fish off the jetties or otherwise use the jetty area are required to have a recreational permit from the base. The recreational possibilities of the interior land are staggering. Locals who enjoy the wilderness take advantage of the excellent fishing and hunting, and others canoe, kayak, and hike for days without seeing another soul. It's only $5.00 for a pass, and another $5.00 for a five-day permit to backcountry camp at your choice of twenty different designated sites.

Perhaps the most pristine and breathtaking 15 miles of coastline in the state of Florida belongs to Eglin, running west along Santa Rosa Island from Fort Walton Beach. Wind-sculpted dunes, as large and varied as anywhere, go on forever. Alas, there is no public access for the entire stretch. It's certainly a beautiful view, though, driving the coast road mile after mile through this sandy emptiness.

ACCESS: From the west on US 98, between Fort Walton Beach and Destin and just before the Destin bridge, turn right out to the beach.

From the east on US 98, just after crossing the bridge out of Destin, turn left out to the beach.

PARKING: Parking lot.

HOURS/FEES: Sunrise–sunset; free. A $5.00 recreational permit for the area around the jetties is available at the Natural Resources Office in Niceville, which is open Monday through Thursday 7:00 A.M.–4:30 P.M., Friday 7:00 A.M.–6:00 P.M., Saturday 7:30 A.M.–12:30 P.M. Closed Sunday and holidays.

AMENITIES: None for the public; Eglin Community Beach Center for military and their families.

ACTIVITIES: Sunbathing, swimming, beach walking, fishing.

FOR MORE INFORMATION: Eglin Air Force Base, Natural Resources Branch (850) 882–4164, 107 Highway 85 North, Niceville, FL 32578.

Beasley/Brackin Wayside Parks—Okaloosa Island Pier

These twin beach parks are the hub of beach life in Okaloosa County. When most of the residents of Fort Walton Beach go out for a day in the sun and sand, this is where they come. Like other sections of the Gulf, the coastal population centers are spread a long way apart, so people looking for a more social beach scene are confined to the rare major public beaches. Beasley and Brackin have every facility imaginable to give them a lively, rocking atmosphere day and night, with a combined sixty-two acres of beach and everything from a dueling-piano nightclub to beach volleyball. At Beasley Park, the 400-seat restaurant Harpoon Hanna's serves up great seafood, and free sunsets drench you in a romantic orange glow.

Brackin Park contains the Okaloosa Island Pier, a local hot spot for fishing and surfing. The Angler's Restaurant and Bar offers a good view of the waves and a respite from the sun. While the pier has been punished mercilessly by hurricanes during the past few decades, the local community is so

Okaloosa Island Pier.

attached to it that it keeps getting rebuilt. In the wake of Hurricane Opal, the pier was raised a few feet in the hope it will endure the next storm better.

ACCESS: From the west on US 98, after crossing bridge from Fort Walton Beach to Santa Rosa Island, Brackin is on your right; Beasley is 0.25 mile farther.

From the east on US 98, after crossing the bridge out of Destin, go 4 miles. Beach parking is on your left for Beasley, and 0.25 mile farther for Brackin.

PARKING: Parking lot.

HOURS/FEES: Sunrise–sunset; free.

AMENITIES: Summer lifeguards, volleyball courts, rest rooms, showers, pavilions, picnic tables, grills, pier, visitor center, 400-seat seafood restaurant, nightclub, playground.

ACTIVITIES: Volleyball, surfing, dining, children's play, fishing, sunbathing, swimming.

FOR MORE INFORMATION: Emerald Coast Visitors Bureau (850) 651–7131 or (800) 322–3319.

Fort Walton Beach Chamber of Commerce (850) 244–8191; http://www.FtWaltonBeach.com.

Beasley Park.

Navarre Beach

Located halfway between Pensacola and Fort Walton Beach, Navarre is far enough off the beaten path that it's stayed a relatively quiet little resort community over the years. Its tranquility was rather rudely shattered by Hurricane Opal in 1995, which lined up Navarre in its sights and blasted it off the face of the map. The relief money actually resulted in the town going through a minor development boom, with people in Pensacola attracted to it as one of the only developable parts of Santa Rosa Island that wasn't owned by the federal government. The Navarre Pier was replaced with a brand-new one, which made surfers and fishermen happy. The pier and the surrounding beach are being converted into a state park scheduled to open by January 2004. Once completed, an entrance fee will be charged, and the hours become 8:00 A.M.–sunset. Lifeguards are on duty during summer months.

One of the casualties of the increased interest in Navarre was the unofficial nude beach down at the east end bordering on Eglin Air Force Base property. After years of tolerance, and naturists advertising Navarre Beach worldwide as a haven for nudists, Santa Rosa County abruptly began cracking down in 1999 by making dozens of arrests. Eglin built a fence to block access to air force property, where the nudists had usually ventured to stay out of range of the $500 antinudity county ordinance (opting for a $70 trespassing fine). These situations come and go, and arrests have been relatively rare lately. Being ready with a wrap usually keeps you out of trouble. Also, it's a good idea to avoid Eglin property during times of heightened national security.

ACCESS: From US 98, midway between Pensacola and Fort Walton Beach, turn south from the town of Navarre onto SR 399. It's 2 miles to the beach.

From Pensacola on SR 399, after crossing the bridge over Pensacola Bay, fork right onto SR 399 and go 20 miles east to Navarre Beach.

PARKING: Parking lot.

HOURS/FEES: Twenty-four hours; free.

AMENITIES: Summer lifeguards, rest rooms, showers, picnic tables.

ACTIVITIES: Surfing, fishing, sunbathing, swimming.

FOR MORE INFORMATION: Navarre Beach Chamber of Commerce (850) 932–7888 or (800) 480–7263.

Named after the devastating hurricane that impacted this section of coast in 1995, Opal Beach provides facilities and parking in the eastern end of the Gulf Islands National Seashore. New picnic shelters are located across a wide beach, and miles of empty strand stretch out on either side. All the tantalizing views of wilderness beach to the east on Eglin Air Force Base property turn into a reality that can now be accessed on the national seashore. But be cautious, sand from the windswept dunes can cascade over the highway. Opal Beach is halfway between Pensacola Beach and Navarre, and well marked.

Closer to Pensacola, the Naval Live Oaks area—which houses the Seashore headquarters—can be found in the town of Gulf Breeze on US 98. Nature trails and picnic areas occupy 1,000 acres of woods and waterfront on

Opal Beach, Gulf Islands National Seashore.

Pensacola Bay. For information about the seashore, especially the historical aspects of the area, this is well worth a visit.

ACCESS: From the east on US 98, midway between Pensacola and Fort Walton Beach, turn left in the town of Navarre onto SR 399 and continue 2 miles to the beach. Turn right onto SR 399 and proceed 7 miles to Opal Beach.

From the west on US 98, after crossing the bridge over Pensacola Bay, fork right onto SR 399 and go 10 miles east to Opal Beach.

PARKING: Parking lot.

HOURS/FEES: 8:00 A.M.–sunset; at Opal Beach, it costs $6.00 per vehicle for a seven-day pass to all Gulf Islands National Seashore locations, $3.00 for a hiker or biker, $20.00 for an annual pass. Free entry with a National Parks Pass or any Golden Pass; all accesses without facilities are free.

AMENITIES: Rest rooms, showers, picnic tables.

ACTIVITIES: Beach walking, sunbathing, swimming, surfing, fishing, picnicking.

FOR MORE INFORMATION: Gulf Islands National Seashore—Naval Live Oaks office (850) 934–2600.

Opal Beach.

Casino Beach

Just when it seems like all there is in the world is the tranquil emerald Gulf and enough sand to fill the Sahara—but a paucity of recreation and other people to recreate with—Casino Beach comes to the rescue. While Sheryl Crow sings of Pensacola's "holy rollers," you won't find their influence here. Casino Beach is acres of tanned flesh in various degrees of skimpy attire. While perhaps not quite the stunning assemblage of beauty that South Beach in Miami is, Casino Beach is nevertheless impressive. Beach volleyball games get played with intensity, sand castles are built, Frisbees fly, and the people who haven't brought coolers to the beach make liberal use of the beachside bars. A curving walkway on the edge of the sand offers in-line skaters and bikers a path to cruise, and circular bleachers every so often offer good perches to check out all the action from.

ACCESS: From US 98, turn south onto SR 399 in the town of Gulf Breeze on the south side of the Pensacola Bay Bridge. It's 2 miles to the beach.

PARKING: Huge parking area.

HOURS/FEES: Twenty-four hours; free.

AMENITIES: Lifeguards, rest rooms, showers, pavilions, amphitheater, picnic tables.

ACTIVITIES: Volleyball, Frisbee, sunbathing, swimming, picnicking.

FOR MORE INFORMATION: Santa Rosa Island Authority (850) 932–2257.

Fort Pickens Gate and East Park

A local secret that people utilize when they want to get away from the crowds of Casino Beach, but still want a free beach, is the beach right before the national seashore gate to Fort Pickens. It has showers and rest rooms, and you can wander freely up and down the beach. There are barbecue grills and numerous picnic shelters, so it's a good lunch spot. Another free facility called East Park at the east end of the community of Pensacola Beach has recently been completed, and it borders on the eastern section of the national seashore on Santa Rosa Island. This gives you a taste of the pristine dune structure of the island, which you lose when you get west to Casino Beach and Fort Pickens.

ACCESS: From US 98, turn south onto SR 399 in the town of Gulf Breeze on the south side of Pensacola Bay Bridge. It's 2 miles to the beach. Turn right and continue 4 miles to just before the entrance to Gulf Islands National Seashore.

PARKING: Parking area.

HOURS/FEES: Twenty-four hours; free.

AMENITIES: Rest rooms, showers, pavilions, picnic tables.

ACTIVITIES: Sunbathing, swimming, picnicking.

FOR MORE INFORMATION: Santa Rosa Island Authority (850) 932–2257.

Langdon Beach/Fort Pickens—Gulf Islands National Seashore

Langdon is the main beach within the Fort Pickens section of the national seashore; it's 2 miles east of the fort itself. It has lifeguards during the summer season, and is a very popular swimming beach. Fort Pickens has a great campground, and gives you a home base to explore all of this area of the park from.

The city of Pensacola went through all the colonial hands the rest of Florida did, with the Spanish, French, and English trying their hands before it was abandoned to pirates and smugglers. Andrew Jackson was finally dispatched to Florida to try to whip it into shape. Fort Pickens was completed in 1834, was held by the Union all through the Civil War, and remained in use until the 1940s. Only the remains exist today, mostly the later concrete additions of gun batteries; little is left of the 21.5 million bricks that went into the original construction.

A pier on Pensacola Bay offers great fishing, and the mouth of the bay occasionally hosts one of the best waves in Florida. Known as Pickens Point, this break helped put Gulf Coast surfing on the map. On big hurricane swells and cold-front swells, when the sandbars are just right and a host of other factors all come together, it is an awesome point break of world-class quality. Unfortunately, the sand hasn't been quite right for a number of years, so

Pier at Pensacola Beach.

Amazons over by Panama City has displaced it as the Gulf's premier big-wave break.

ACCESS: From US 98, turn south onto SR 399 in the town of Gulf Breeze on the south side of Pensacola Bay Bridge and continue 2 miles to the beach. Turn right (west) onto SR 399 and drive 7 miles.

PARKING: Parking lot.

HOURS/FEES: 8:00 A.M.–sunset; it's $6.00 per vehicle for a seven-day pass to all Gulf Islands National Seashore locations, $3.00 for a hiker or biker, $20.00 for an annual pass. Free entry with a National Parks Pass or any Golden Pass.

AMENITIES: Summer lifeguards, campground, rest rooms, showers, pavilions, picnic tables, historic fort ruins.

ACTIVITIES: Historic touring, surfing, beach walking, sunbathing, swimming, fishing, picnicking.

FOR MORE INFORMATION: Gulf Islands National Seashore—Fort Pickens Visitors Center (850) 934–2635.

Johnson Beach—Gulf Islands National Seashore

The section of the national seashore on Perdido Key is named after Rosamond Johnson, the first black serviceman to die in the Korean War. From where Johnson Beach Road ends, the beach runs on for 5 miles to Pensacola Pass, all of which is accessible only by foot or boat. The seclusion of the outer margins has made it popular both as a nude beach and as a gay beach. The beach is gorgeous, with rolling dunes and powdery white sand. There are summer lifeguards at the parking area beach.

Primitive camping is allowed anywhere on the wilderness section farther than a half mile from the parking area, though a permit is required if you're going to leave a vehicle overnight. Fires can be built as long as they're on the beach below the high-tide line. If you don't mind roughing it a bit, this is a good way to enjoy a romantic adventure.

The park does get quite busy during summer months, when many families from Mississippi and Alabama are taking their vacations, but through the rest of the year it's pretty quiet. At all times of year, the half-mile rule applies: Walk for more than a half mile and you'll leave most of humanity behind. Do be careful about bringing enough water and sun protection for long walks, though. Soft sand gets to feel like quicksand eventually.

ACCESS: From US 98 in downtown Pensacola, take SR 292 south 15 miles to Perdido Key. Turn left onto Johnson Beach Road to parking.

PARKING: Parking lot.

HOURS/FEES: 8:00 A.M.–sunset; it costs $6.00 per vehicle for a seven-day pass to all Gulf Islands National Seashore locations, $3.00 for a hiker or biker, $20.00 for an annual pass. Free entry with a National Parks Pass or any Golden Pass.

AMENITIES: Summer lifeguards, summer snack bar, campground, rest rooms, showers, pavilions, picnic tables, nature trail.

ACTIVITIES: Beach walking, sunbathing, swimming, fishing, hiking, picnicking, primitive camping.

FOR MORE INFORMATION: Gulf Islands National Seashore—Fort Barrancas Visitor Center (850) 455–5167.

Perdido Key State Park

West of the national seashore, close to the border of Alabama, this is the westernmost public beach in the Panhandle. Just as Fort Clinch provides a beautiful first look at Florida's beaches on the state's east coast, Perdido Key offers a gorgeous first look coming from Alabama. The pristine dunes of bright white sand, covered with clumps of sea oats, contrast with the deep blue sea. There are relatively minimal facilities, but hundreds of acres of undeveloped wild Florida to enjoy. Aside from rest rooms and showers, what else do you really need when you have a beach this pretty?

The name *Perdido Key* means "lost island," which doesn't apply well to the overdeveloped island community of the same name, but is perfect for the state park and national seashore sections. *Boating World* magazine named the key as one of the top one hundred "fantasy islands" for boaters; it also has fared well in other national rankings of top beaches.

ACCESS: From US 98, in downtown Pensacola, take SR 292 south 17 miles to the park entrance.

Perdido Key State Park.

From Alabama on SR 292, just inside the Florida border, look for the parking area on your right.

PARKING: Parking lot.

HOURS/FEES: 8:00 A.M.–sunset; $2.00.

AMENITIES: Rest rooms, showers, picnic pavilion.

ACTIVITIES: Beach walking, sunbathing, swimming, fishing, picnicking.

FOR MORE INFORMATION: Perdido Key State Park (850) 492–1595.

Sea oats.

Ghost Crabs

One of the ubiquitous creatures of Florida's sandy beaches is the ghost crab, a fleet-footed creature that blends in perfectly with its surroundings. Often you'll see no more than a blur of movement across the sand, which looks almost like a hallucination since you can't see exactly what it is that's moving. If you're out on a wilderness beach at dawn, you might be lucky enough to observe the odd phenomenon my mother has seen: Night herons standing patiently over ghost crab holes, absolutely still, waiting for them to come out. With a sudden strike of the beak—voilà!—they have one. Not blessed with the gigantic throat of the pelican, or even the gullet of giraffe-necked great blue herons, the night heron then discovers that the ghost crab is a bit much to handle all at once. They try to swallow the body anyway, which sticks in their throat and perplexes them to no end. Still, it can be worse for them. The herons that simply stab with a closed beak can find a crab impaled on it, leaving them unable to open their mouths.

As a youngster, my oldest brother, Jim, took part in the first Great Ghost Crab Race in the nation. Dreamed up as a promotional idea for a new airline route and cosponsored by the Miami Seaquarium, the race took place at the Seaquarium with a $50 savings bond going to the winner. Jim was scared of his crab—the overcoming of that fear, along with the exultation of seeing his crab race to victory, faded when he was confronted with TV cameras and everyone's attention. At that point he burst into tears. It didn't help that he was the grandson of the promoter. Luckily the sport was new enough that no one could even speculate on how you could fix a ghost crab race. One child was a little miffed that his crab refused to budge from the starting position. And no one demanded the crabs be drug-tested.

Index

A

Air Force Armament Museum, 135
Amazons, 110
Anclote Keys, 71
Anclote Keys Preserve State Park, 72,
    77–78
Angler's Restaurant and Bar, 139
Apalachicola, 85
Apalachicola Seafood Festival, 87
Australian pine, xiv–xv

B

Bailey-Matthews Shell Museum,
    23–24
Barbara B. Mann Performing Arts
    Hall and Gallery, 23
Barefoot Beach Preserve, 15–16
Bay County Pier, 111–12
beach mice, 127
Beasley Park, 139–40
Big Bend, 71–72
Big Cypress National Preserve, 4, 20
Big Lagoon State Park, 135
birding, 77
Blackwater River State Park, 135
Blind Pass Beach, 33–34
Blue Mountain Beach, 124
Blue Springs, 82
Blue Springs Lake, 82
Boca Grande, 29
Boca Grande Pass, 21
Boston Red Sox Spring Training, 23
bottlenose dolphins, 110, 115–16

Bowditch Point Regional Park, 19
Bowman's Beach, 26–27
Brackin Wayside Park, 139–40
Briggs Nature Center, The, 4
Broadway Palm Dinner Theatre, 23
Brocato, Tom, 92–93
Brohard Park, 42–43
Broke-a-Toe, 92–93
Brown, Loren "Totch," 8
Butcher, Clyde, 28
butterflies, Monarch, 98
Byars, "Trader Frank" and Jo, 64

C

Café on the Beach, 50
Caladesi Island State Park, 56, 57,
    67–68
Calusa Nature Center and
    Planetarium, 23
Camp Helen State Park, 114
Cape Palms Park, 95–96
Cape Sable, 7–8
Cape San Blas Camping Resort, 86
Cape San Blas Lighthouse, 96
Cape St. George Lighthouse, 91
Cape St. George State Reserve,
    86, 91
Captiva Beach, 27–28
Captiva Island, 21, 36
Casino Beach, 144
Caspersen Beach, 41
casuarina, xiv–xv
Cayo Costa Island, 21

Cayo Costa State Park, 22, 28–29
Cedar Key, 72, 80
Cedar Keys National Wildlife
    Refuge, 80–81
Chassahowitzka Springs/National
    Wildlife Refuge, 74, 83
Chokolosee, 8
Citrus County Chassahowitzka River
    Campground, 73
City Pier, 112–13
Ciumba, 115–16
Civil War, 51, 83
Clam Pass County Park, 13–14
Clearwater Marine Science Center
    Aquarium, 58
Clyde Butcher Gallery, 4
Collier County Historical Museum, 4
Collier-Seminole State Park, 3, 4
Conservancy of Southwest Florida's
    Briggs Nature Center, The, 4
Coquina Beach, 49
coquina rock, xv
Corkscrew Swamp Sanctuary,
    5, 20
Cortez Beach, 49
crabs, ghost, 151
Crab Trap, 128
CR30A Scenic Bike Trail, 119
Crooked Inlet East, 106–7
Crooked Inlet West, 108
Crooked River Lighthouse, 87, 89
Crystal River, 83
Crystal River National Wildlife
    Refuge, 79
Crystal River State Archaeological
    Site, 73–74

D

deer, sambra, 99
Deer Lake State Park, 121–22
Delnor-Wiggins Pass State Park,
    14–15
De Soto National Memorial, 39
Destin, 117–18
Destin Fishing Museum, The, 119
Dog Island, 89
dolphins, bottlenose, 110, 115–16
Don Pedro Island, 21
Don Pedro Island State Park, 30

E

Eagle Pencils, 80
eastern diamondback rattlesnakes, 67
East Park, 144–45
Econfina Creek, 103
Econfina River State Park, 74
Eden State Gardens and Museum,
    119, 121
Edison-Ford Winter Estates, 23
Ed Walline Park, 125–26
Eglin Air Force Base, 133, 134, 138
Egmont Key State Park, 51–52
Englewood, 21
Englewood Beach, 32–33
Everglades National Park, 1, 3, 4

F

Fakahatchee Strand State Preserve,
    4–5, 20
Flamingo Campground, 3
Florida Aquarium, The, 57
Fort Dade, 51
Fort De Soto County Park, 56, 60

Fort Island Beach, 79
Fort Myers, 21
Fort Myers Beach, 1–2
Fort Myers Historical
    Museum, 23
Fort Myers KOA, 22
Fort Panic Park, 126
Fort Pickens, 145–47
Fort Pickens Campground, 134
Fort Pickens Gate, 144–45
Frog Creek Campground and RV
    Park, 38

G

Gasparilla, Jose, 53
Gasparilla Island State Park, 21,
    29–30
Gay, Tommy and Robert, 99
ghost crabs, 151
Gomez, Johnny, 53
gopher tortoises, 67
"Grandpa's Wharves," 49
Grayton Beach, 117
Grayton Beach State Park, 118,
    122–23
Gulfarium, 135
Gulf Beach Campground, 38
Gulf Breeze Zoo, 135
Gulf Islands National Seashore, 134,
    142–43, 145–48
Gulf World Aquarium, 103

H

Hanna, Roy S., 61
Harpoon Hanna's, 139
Hatch, George, 99

Henderson Beach State Park, 118–19,
    129–30
Hermitage, 33
Hickory Landing, 86
Hodges Park, 82
Hog Island, 68
Homosassa Springs State Wildlife
    Park, 73, 83
Honeymoon Island, 68
Honeymoon Island State Park, 68–69
Howard Park, 76
Hurricane Island, 108

I

iguanas, 29
Indian Shores Access, 64–65
Indian Temple Mound Museum and
    Park, 135
Inlet Beach, 121
Island Hotel, 80

J

Jackson, Andrew, 145
James Lee County Park, 128–29
jellyfish, xiii
J. N. "Ding" Darling National
    Wildlife Refuge, 21, 24, 26
John Gorrie Museum, 87
Johnson, Rosamond, 147
Johnson Beach, 134, 147–48
John's Pass, 62
John's Pass Beach, 62–63

K

Keaton Beach, 82
Keaton Beach Campground, 73

Killing Mr. Watson, 8

Koreshan State Historic Site, 5

L

Lalla, 115–16

Langdon Beach, 145–47

Lee County Alliance of the Arts, 23

LeeTran trolley, 18

Lido Beach, 48

Lido Beach Casino, 48

Little Manatee River State Park, 56

Little St. George Island, 91

Loomis brothers, 99

Lovers Key State Park, 17

Lowdermilk Beach, 12

Lowry Park Zoological Garden, 57

Lynn Hall Park, 18

M

Madeira Beach, 62–63

Madeira Beach Resort KOA, 57

Manasota Beach, 35

Manasota Key, 21, 33

Manatee Beach, 50–51

manatees, West Indian, 79, 83

Manatee Springs State Park, 73

Marco Island, 1

Marco Island KOA, 3–4

Marie Selby Botanical Gardens, 39

Matanzas Pass Wilderness Preserve, 5

Matthiessen, Peter, 8

Megalodon shark, 53

Mexico Beach, 101, 105–6

mice, beach, 127

Monarch butterflies, 98

Morey, Selwyn, 61

Morris, Sippi, 20

Mote Marine Aquarium, 37, 38–39

"Mullet Express," 83

Museum of African-American Art, The, 57

Museum of Science and Industry, The, 57

Museum of the Islands, 23

Myakka River, 32

Myakka River State Park and Wilderness Preserve, 22, 38, 39

N

Naples, 1

Naples KOA, 3–4

Naples Pier, 11–12

Naples Swamp Buggy Race, 20

Naples Visitor Center, 11

Naval Live Oaks area, 142–43

Navarre, 133

Navarre Beach, 141

North Captiva Island, 21

North Jetty Beach, 43–44

North Jetty Park, 37

North Lido Beach, 48

nudity, xiv, 131, 141

O

Ochlockonee River State Park, 87

Okaloosa Island Pier, 133, 139–40

Old Destin Post Office, 119

Opal Beach, 142–43

Oscar Scherer State Park, 38, 39

Owl Creek, 86

P

Palm Cottage, 5

Palmer Point Beach, 44–45

Palooza, 115–16

Panama City, 101

Panama City Beach, 101, 112–13

Panama City Beach KOA, 102

Panama City Beach Visitors
    Center, 103

Pass-a-Grille Beach, 61

Patio Café, 49

Pavilion Key, 8

Peace River, 53

Pelican Inn, 89

Pelican Pier, 18

Pensacola, 145

Pensacola Beach, 133

Pensacola Museum of Art, 136

Pensacola Naval Air Station, 135–36

Perdido Key State Park, 148–50

pet beaches, 68

Philharmonic Center for the Arts,
    The, 5

Pickens Point, 145

Pierce, Dr., 99

Pier Park, 112

Pine Island KOA, 22

Pine Log State Forest, 102–3

porpoises, 110, 115–16

R

rattlesnakes, eastern diamondback, 67

Red Coconut RV Court on the
    Beach, 4

red tide, xiii

red wolves, 99

Reno, Janet, 20

Ringling, John, 48

Ringling Museum of Art, 39

Roser, Charles, 37

Rustic Sands Resort
    Campground, 102

S

safety, xiii–xiv

Salinas Park, 94

Salvador Dali Museum, The, 58

sambra deer, 99

San Carlos RV Park & Islands, 4

Sand Dollar Island, 9

sand fleas, 70

Sand Key County Park, 66

Sanibel Island, 21, 36

Sanibel Lighthouse, 19, 26

Sanibel Lighthouse Boardwalk, 24

"Sanibel Stoop," 36

San Marcos de Apalache State His-
    toric Site, 74

Santa Rosa Island, 133

Sarasota, 37

scalloping, 82

Seahorse Key, 81

sea oats, xiv

seashells, 36

Seaside, 117

sea turtles, xv

Seminole Gulf Railway, 23

Seminole Wars, 81

sharks, xiii

sharks, Megalodon, 53

shark's teeth, 53

Sharks Tooth Festival, 43

Sharky's Restaurant, 42
shelling, 36
Shell Island, 109–10
Siesta Key Beach Park, 46–47
Sippi Super-Suction Snakebite
    System, 20
slash pine, 68
Spanish-American War, 51
St. Andrews State Park, 102, 109–10
St. George Island State Park, 86, 90
St. Joseph Peninsula State Park, 86,
    97–98
St. Petersburg KOA, 57
St. Vincent National Wildlife Refuge,
    92–93
Stump Pass Beach State Park, 31–32
Suncoast Seabird Sanctuary, The, 58
Sunset Isles RV Park, 73
swamps, 20

T

Tampa Bay, 55
Tampa Museum of Art, The, 58
Teddy Bear Museum of Naples,
    The, 5
Ten Thousand Islands, 8–9
Thousand Island salad dressing, 8
Tigertail Beach County Park, 9–10
Tiki Gardens, 64–65
Topsail Hill State Preserve, 127
Topsail Hill State Preserve RV
    Resort, 118
tortoises, gopher, 67

Totch, 8
Treasure Island Beach, 62
Truman Show, The, 117
turpentine, 91, 110
Turtle Beach, 44–45
turtles, sea, xv
Tyndall Air Force Base, 101, 106–8
Tyndall Beach, 108

U

Useppa Museum, The, 24

V

Venice, 37
Venice Pier, 42–43

W

Waccasassa Bay State Preserve, 73, 74
Warm Mineral Springs, 39
West Indian manatees, 79, 83
Wilderness Waterway, 8
Willoughby, Hugh, 7
wolves, red, 99
World War II, 68

Y

Ybor City Brewing Company, The,
    57–58
Ybor City Museum, The, 58
Yulee, David Levy, 80, 83
Yulee Sugar Mill Ruins State Historic
    Site, 74